The New York Times

PUBLIC PROFILES

Pope Francis

EDUCATIONAL PUBLISHING BOOKS

THE NEW YORK TIMES EDITORIAL STAFF

Published in 2019 by New York Times Educational Publishing
in association with The Rosen Publishing Group, Inc.
29 East 21st Street, New York, NY 10010

First Edition

The New York Times
Alex Ward: Editorial Director, Book Development
Phyllis Collazo: Photo Rights/Permissions Editor
Heidi Giovine: Administrative Manager

Rosen Publishing
Megan Kellerman: Managing Editor
Michael Hessel-Mial: Editor
Greg Tucker: Creative Director
Brian Garvey: Art Director

Cataloging-in-Publication Data
Names: New York Times Company.
Title: Pope Francis / edited by the New York Times editorial staff.
Description: New York : New York Times Educational Publishing, 2019. | Series: Public profiles | Includes glossary and index.
Identifiers: ISBN 9781642821727 (library bound) | ISBN 9781642821710 (pbk.) | ISBN 9781642821734 (ebook)
Subjects: LCSH: Francis, Pope, 1936—Juvenile literature. | Popes—Biography—Juvenile literature.
Classification: LCC BX1378.7 P674 2019 | DDC 282.092 B—dc23

Manufactured in the United States of America

On the cover: Pope Francis conducts an open-air Mass at Benjamin Franklin Parkway in Philadelphia, Sept. 27, 2015. The Mass, which was expected to draw about one million people, concluded the Vatican-sponsored World Meeting of Families; Damon Winter/The New York Times.

Contents

CHAPTER 3

The Church, Social Issues and a Changing World

CHAPTER 4

The Pope as International Actor

CHAPTER 5

The Challenge of Reforming a Church in Crisis

Introduction

FOR MUCH OF THE 2,000 YEARS of Christianity's history, the Roman Catholic Church has been a symbol of the religion's influence and core doctrine. Playing a pivotal role in world history since its adoption by the Roman Empire, the church has also drawn criticism for its adherence to tradition and use of power. As a visible symbol of this church in a changing world, the actions of the pope are heavily scrutinized for religious and political significance. Pope Francis, head of the church since 2013, is no exception. His papacy has been characterized by a strong will to modernize, a commitment to social justice, a conservative backlash and a struggle to resolve the church's more entrenched challenges.

Elected after the resignation of his predecessor Benedict XVI, Francis inherited a church in disarray. The church's finances were in question and the often obscure inner workings of church politics were being leaked to the public. The influence of the church was starting to wane in the Western world. Most importantly, sexual abuse of children by priests, spanning decades and hidden by church authorities, was finally being reported and exposed. As sharp criticism of the church mounted, the new pope was not only tasked with steering the church through crisis, but with justifying its relevance beyond the Catholic world.

Pope Francis, born Mario Bergoglio before assuming his papal name, is the first Latin American pope and the first pope from the Jesuit order. As cardinal in Argentina, Bergoglio was a cultural conservative and economic progressive. He clashed with the Argentine president by upholding the church's opposition to birth control, homosexuality and abortion, while also criticizing social inequality. In this, Cardinal Bergoglio was in line with most of the progressive wing of the Catholic church.

RICHARD PERRY/THE NEW YORK TIMES

People sign a drawing of Francis following a speech he gave in Philadelphia during his visit to America in September 2015.

As pope, Francis quickly earned a reputation for humility, choosing simpler dress and refusing to reside in the traditionally elaborate lodgings of earlier popes. He also quickly established social justice as a core theme of his papacy, making statements criticizing capitalism and the destruction of the environment. Francis reversed Benedict XVI's more reclusive role by weighing in on global events, visiting conflict regions and criticizing rising authoritarianism.

Some of the greatest surprises of Francis' papacy have been his progressivism on social issues. In establishing his concerns with economic inequality, he quickly shifted the priorities of the church's teachings. While not changing official church doctrine, Francis has given individual parishes greater leeway in ordaining openly gay priests and administering communion to divorcées. While the church officially holds right of center doctrinal positions on issues relating to sexuality and the family, Francis' papacy has signaled an openness in actual practice.

Despite wide beliefs that the pope has unlimited power within the church, Francis has not gone without criticism from other church leaders. Francis' openness on social issues has sparked larger tensions on the future of the church in a changing world. These tensions have been inflamed by the pope's choice to demote several powerful conservative cardinals, leading some to conclude that Francis was forcing his progressive views on the church. American Catholics, many of whom have aligned with conservative politics in recent decades, have been especially critical of the church's leftward shift.

While Francis' positions have been controversial, no other issue has lost the church more esteem than the ongoing revelations of sexual abuse. While sexual abuse of children by priests has been public knowledge since the early 2000s, the scope and the church's willing protection of abusive priests threaten to undermine the goodwill generated by Francis' social justice messaging. Despite achieving moderate reforms elsewhere in the Vatican, Francis has been slow, if not reluctant, to address abuse issues. Francis eventually mollified critics by thoroughly investigating an especially widespread abuse case in Chile, but more and more cases of systemic abuse continue to appear. A grand jury report revealing the graphic sexual abuse of thousands of children in Pennsylvania brought these issues to a fever pitch. Many of Francis' critics have called for his resignation in the wake of his alleged protection of abuser priests.

Unlike other controversies of Francis' papacy, the child abuse issue erodes the pope's strongest asset: his global image of leading the church into the 21st century. Where Francis' struggles against the conservative faction of the church could be seen as a badge of pride for progressives, protection of abuse is seen as driving the faithful of all political stripes away. Pope Francis positioned himself as capable of reconciling the church's past with its future by the force of his personality. As the church continues to reel from the outcry over abused children, its longstanding problems threaten to exceed the powers of Catholicism's most-watched leader.

CHAPTER 1

The Election of Pope Francis

Poor health and a series of scandals at the Vatican led Pope Benedict XVI to resign less than eight years after his election. The first papal resignation since 1415, the announcement exposed internal Vatican conflicts over the Papal State's finances, sexual abuse and internal disorder over social issues. Cardinal Mario Bergoglio, a contender in the previous papal conclave, was elected, and he adopted the name Francis. Considered a social conservative with a bent for reform, Bergoglio quickly broke from Vatican traditions with public expressions of personal humility.

A Statement Rocks Rome, Then Sends Shockwaves Around the World

BY RACHEL DONADIO AND NICHOLAS KULISH | FEB. 11, 2013

VATICAN CITY — The decision, delivered in Latin and in unemotional tones by Pope Benedict XVI to a gathering of cardinals on Monday, came "like a bolt out of the blue," one of the participants said, and it soon ricocheted around the world.

During what was supposed to be a routine meeting to discuss the canonization of three potential saints, Benedict read a statement that said, in part, that after examining his conscience "before God, I have come to the certainty that my strengths, due to an advanced age, are no longer suited to an adequate exercise" of leading the world's one billion Roman Catholics. He was resigning on Feb. 28, he said, becoming the first pope to do so in six centuries.

"In today's world," Benedict said in his announcement, "subject to so many rapid changes and shaken by questions of deep relevance for the life of faith, in order to govern the bark of St. Peter and proclaim the gospel, both strength of mind and body are necessary, strength which in the last few months has deteriorated in me to the extent that I have had to recognize my incapacity to adequately fulfill the ministry entrusted to me."

Within minutes, #Pontifexit was trending on Twitter. Later, during an evening thunderstorm, a lightning bolt struck the dome of St. Peter's, though the meaning, if any, was not immediately clear.

In recent months, Benedict, 85, had been showing signs of age. He often seemed tired and even appeared to doze off during Midnight Mass on Christmas Eve, after being taken to the altar of Saint Peter's on a wheeled platform. But few expected the pope to resign so suddenly, even though he had said in the past that he would consider the option.

"The pope took us by surprise," said the Vatican spokesman, the Rev. Federico Lombardi, expounding on one of the most dramatic moments in centuries of Vatican history. He appeared at a hastily called news conference on Monday, where he sat alone at a table, with an unopened bottle of mineral water and a dog-eared copy of a Canon Law guide before him.

Father Lombardi said the pope did not display strong emotions as he made his announcement, but spoke with "great dignity, great concentration and great understanding of the significance of the moment."

In a statement, President Obama recalled meeting with Benedict in 2009. "I have appreciated our work together over these last four years," the president said. "The church plays a critical role in the United States and the world, and I wish the best to those who will soon gather to choose His Holiness Pope Benedict XVI's successor."

Prime Minister Mario Monti of Italy called Benedict's decision "immense and unexpected."

More than a few observers were struck that such a traditionalist as Benedict would make such an unconventional exit. "A departure that is paradoxically modern for a pope who was so conservative," said Christian Terras, the founder and executive editor of Golias, a religious review near Lyon, France, that has been critical of the Catholic Church.

Some said that Benedict's decision to step down was one of the most dramatic acts in the history of the papacy. "This decision has been the only great reform of Benedict, and at the same time it is a revolutionary step for the Catholic Church," said Marco Politi, a Vatican expert and author of a book on Benedict's papacy. While in past centuries, popes had stepped down over political struggles, Mr. Politi said, "this is a clear decision and a free decision made by the pope that will set an example also for the future, setting a limit for the pontificate."

Benedict's 89-year-old brother, the Rev. Georg Ratzinger, said that the pope's weakening health had led him to step down. "His age was taking its toll," Father Ratzinger told the German news agency DPA on Monday, adding that he had been aware of his brother's plan for several months.

That the resignation was long in the planning was confirmed by Giovanni Maria Vian, the editor of the Vatican newspaper, L'Osservatore Romano, who wrote on Monday that the pope's decision "was taken many months ago," after his trip to Mexico and Cuba in March 2012, "and kept with a reserve that no one could violate."

Father Lombardi said that the pope would retire first to his summer residence in Castel Gandolfo, in the hills outside Rome, and later to a monastery in Vatican City.

Benedict, the former Cardinal Joseph Ratzinger, was elected on April 19, 2005. At the time, Benedict was a popular choice within the college of 115 cardinals who chose him as a man who shared — and at times went beyond — the conservative theology of his predecessor and mentor, John Paul II, and seemed ready to take over the job after serving beside him for more than two decades.

The church's 265th pope, Benedict was the first German to hold the title in half a millennium, and his election was a milestone toward Germany's spiritual renewal 60 years after World War II and the Holocaust. At 78, he was also the oldest pope to be elected since 1730.

But Benedict was seen as a weak manager, and his papacy was troubled by debilitating scandals, most recently when his butler was convicted by a Vatican court in October of aggravated theft after he admitted stealing confidential documents, many of which wound up in a tell-all book that showed behind-the-scenes Vatican intrigue.

Benedict "centered his papacy on giving faith to Christians, focusing on the essence of what it means to be a Christian, and he managed to do it in spite of the fact that his communicative capacities weren't so brilliant," Sandro Magister, a Vatican expert, said. "Most common people, I don't mean intellectuals, saw him as a disinterested man who spent all his life for a high cause, which was to revive the faith."

At first blush, criticism was muted for a pope with a controversial term, marred by child-abuse scandals and growing discord over conservative stances on issues like divorce and women in the clergy.

Hans Küng, a theologian and former colleague of Benedict's who is now one of his most articulate critics, called his decision to step down "understandable for many reasons," according to the dpa news service, but added that so many conservative cardinals had been named during his tenure, it would be difficult to find someone "who could lead the church out of its multifaceted crisis."

The strongest criticism came from the victims of clerical sexual abuse, who faulted Benedict for failing to take stronger steps or, in some eyes, any steps at all.

"This pope had a great opportunity to finally address the decades of abuse in the church, but at the end of the day he did nothing but promise everything and in the end he ultimately delivered nothing," John Kelly, of the support group Survivors of Child Abuse, told Agence France-Presse.

Tom Cronin of Irish Survivors of Institutional Abuse International said that while age and infirmity were given as reasons for the pope's resignation, he believed the continuing clerical abuse scandal had played a part.

"I don't think he has been able to deal with it, and it was probably the straw that broke his back," Mr. Cronin said. "Every day we still get revelations about this priest or that bishop, and maybe he wasn't young enough to confront it and perhaps, too, he hasn't been getting the right advice. Whatever the reason, the church hierarchy just hasn't faced up to the atrocities and their denials and inaction continue to damage them."

In Rome, where souvenir shops often carry more postcards of John Paul than of Benedict, news of Benedict's resignation was met with surprise and some sadness. "Anyone could tell that he was old and sick, and that such a complicated situation like the one he has to face is a lot, but I had never heard that a pope could quit," said Simonetta Piersanti, 52, a cleaning woman in a residence run by nuns.

She mentioned a common Roman saying, "When a pope dies, they just elect another," which captures the lack of excitement with which Italians greet historic events. "We'll have to do it even without the death part," she added.

RACHEL DONADIO reported from Vatican City, and **NICHOLAS KULISH** from Berlin. Reporting was contributed by **ALAN COWELL** in London, **DOUGLAS DALBY** in Dublin, **DOREEN CARVAJAL** in Paris, and **ELISABETTA POVOLEDO** and **GAIA PIANIGIANI** in Rome.

Successor to Benedict Will Lead a Church at a Crossroads

BY RACHEL DONADIO AND ELISABETTA POVOLEDO | FEB. 11, 2013

VATICAN CITY — Pope Benedict XVI's surprise announcement on Monday that he will resign on Feb. 28 sets the stage for a succession battle that is likely to determine the future course of a church troubled by scandal and declining faith in its traditional strongholds around the world.

Citing advanced years and infirmity, Benedict became the first pope in six centuries to resign. Vatican officials said they hoped to have a new pope in place by Easter, while expressing shock at a decision that some said had been made as long as a year ago.

Saying he had examined his conscience "before God," Benedict said he felt that he was not up to the challenge of guiding the world's one billion Catholics. That task will fall to his successor, who will have to contend not only with a Roman Catholic Church marred by the sexual abuse crisis, but also with an increasingly secular Europe and the spread of Protestant evangelical movements in the United States, Latin America and Africa.

The resignation sets up a struggle between the staunchest conservatives, in Benedict's mold, who advocate a smaller church of more fervent believers, and those who believe that the church can broaden its appeal in small but significant ways, like allowing divorced Catholics who remarry without an annulment to receive communion or loosening restrictions on condom use in an effort to prevent AIDS. There are no plausible candidates who would move on issues like ending celibacy for priests, or the ordination of women.

Many Vatican watchers suspect that the cardinals will choose someone with better management skills and a more personal touch than the bookish Benedict, someone who can extend the church's reach to new constituencies, particularly to the young people of Europe, for whom the church is now largely irrelevant, and to Latin America and Africa, where evangelical movements are fast encroaching.

"They want somebody who can carry this idea of new evangelization, relighting the missionary fires of the church and actually make it work, not just lay it out in theory," said John L. Allen, a Vatican expert at the National Catholic Reporter and author of many books on the papacy. Someone who will be "the church's missionary in chief, a showman and salesman for the Catholic faith, who can take the reins of government more personally into his own hands," he added.

The other big battle in the church is over the demographic distribution of Catholics, which has shifted decisively to the developing world. Today, 42 percent of adherents come from Latin America, and about 15 percent from Africa, versus only 25 percent from Europe. That has led many in the church to say that the new pope should represent a part of the world where membership is growing quickly, while others say that spiritual vision should be paramount.

But while most of the world's Catholics live outside Europe, most of the cardinals come from Europe, pointing to a central tension: while the Vatican is a global organization, it is often run like an Italian village.

Under normal circumstances, the cardinals would descend on Rome after the death of the reigning pope. In this case, said the Vatican spokesman, the Rev. Federico Lombardi, the pope will carry out his duties until Feb. 28 at 8 p.m., with a successor probably elected by Easter, which this year falls on March 31. But he said the timing for an election of a new pope was "not an announcement, it's a hypothesis."

Already, speculation is rife about who best fills the perceived needs of the church. Cardinal Angelo Scola, the powerful archbishop of Milan, is seen as the strongest Italian contender. A conservative theologian with an interest in bioethics and Catholic-Muslim relations, he is known for his intellect, his background in the same theological tradition as Benedict, his media savvy and his strong ties with the Italian political establishment. Vatican experts laud his popular touch, even if his writings are often opaque.

Cardinal Marc Ouellet, a dogmatic theologian and a Canadian, is widely seen as a favorite of Benedict, who named him head of the Vatican's influential Congregation for Bishops to help select bishops around the world. Critics in his native Quebec said that he was out of step with the province's more progressive bishops, but that is not necessarily a drawback in today's church.

Cardinal Peter Appiah Turkson of Ghana, the head of the Vatican's Pontifical Council for Social Justice, is seen as the most likely African contender for the papacy. Educated in Rome and New York, he is known for his semiorthodox views on the use of condoms, saying that married couples could possibly use them to prevent infection when one partner is H.I.V.-positive, although he has also defended Pope Benedict's remark that condom use increases the risk of AIDS spreading.

Cardinal Leonardo Sandri, the prefect for the Congregation for Eastern Churches, is an Argentine, who would excite the Latin American wing of the church. He is also a skillful Vatican insider who served in the Secretariat of State under John Paul II and knows how to navigate the Vatican's complex bureaucracy, which might make him effective, Vatican experts say.

During the cold war it would have been a long shot, but for the first time there is talk that an American, Cardinal Timothy M. Dolan of New York, could be a contender for pope. His deep conservatism combined with a folksy charisma make him popular with the faithful, at a time when the church is focused on "new evangelization."

Benedict was seen as a weak manager, and his papacy was troubled by debilitating scandals, most recently one in which his butler was convicted by a Vatican court in October of aggravated theft after he admitted stealing confidential documents, many of which wound up in a tell-all book that showed behind-the-scenes Vatican intrigue.

His successor will have to contend with a range of staggering practical challenges, including a perennial shortage of priests and nuns worldwide, as well as a sexual abuse crisis that has undermined the church's moral authority, especially in Germany and the English-speaking countries where it has been most aggressively discovered.

"I'd say the biggest challenge was the collapse of Catholic numbers across Europe," where "Christianity is in such free-fall in former Catholic countries, that the prognosis is not good," said Philip Jenkins, distinguished professor of history at the Institute for Studies of Religion at Baylor University, in Waco, Tex., citing Ireland as a particularly telling case.

In much of the developing world, especially Latin America — which accounts for half of the world's Catholics — and parts of Africa, evangelical churches are moving in on territory once dominated by the Catholic Church, drawing in new faithful with services that offer upbeat music and an emphasis on self-improvement.

"If I were investing the church's efforts, I would put Latin American high, to avoid a second Europe," Mr. Jenkins said.

But the church's concern about the developing world will not necessarily lead to the selection of a pope from that part of the world, Vatican experts said.

Pope Benedict has appointed 67 cardinals and of these, 37 are from Europe, which remains the most substantial voting block, and potentially the most influential.

Nearly all of the 117 cardinals who will vote for the new pope were appointed by Benedict and his predecessor, John Paul II, both strong traditionalists, and it is likely that the next pope will share their vision and doctrine.

With more than 150 million Catholics and a rapidly growing population, Africa represents one of the church's few avenues for expansion, and church leaders have assiduously promoted charismatic bishops and cardinals in nations with substantial Catholic populations, like Nigeria and Ghana.

In 2002, Benedict, then Cardinal Joseph Ratzinger, spoke of the merits of electing an African pope. "For all its condemnation of racism, the Western world still has reservations about the third world," he said then. "Yet, in Africa for example, we have truly great figures whom we can only admire. They are fully up to the job."

But most Vatican experts said that was not likely. "There's a very strong likelihood that it will be someone from Europe," said the Rev. Thomas J. Reese, senior fellow at the Woodstock Theological Center, at Georgetown University.

The Vatican spokesman, Father Lombardi, said Monday that after Feb. 28, the pope would retire from public view and would not participate in the appointment of his successor. But many wondered whether his presence would have an impact. "The fact is that he's alive, and it's obvious that his opinion, his perception will be felt," said Paolo Rodari, a Vatican reporter for the daily Il Foglio.

NICHOLAS KULISH contributed reporting from Berlin, and **ALAN COWELL** from London.

The End of a Catholic Moment

OPINION | BY ROSS DOUTHAT | FEB. 16, 2013

THE LAST TIME the Chair of St. Peter stood vacant, during Pope John Paul II's funeral in 2005, the Roman Catholic Church enjoyed a wave of unusually favorable coverage from the American press. The Polish pope had a way of disarming even his most stringent critics, and that power extended beyond his death, turning his funeral into a made-for-television spectacle that almost felt like an infomercial for the Catholic faith.

Perhaps not coincidentally, the mid-2000s were the last time the Catholic vision of the good society — more egalitarian than American conservatism and more moralistic than American liberalism — enjoyed real influence in U.S. politics. At the time of John Paul's death, the Republican Party's agenda was still stamped by George W. Bush's "compassionate conservatism," which offered a right-of-center approach to Catholic ideas about social justice. The Democratic Party, meanwhile, was looking for ways to woo the "values voters" (many of them Catholic) who had just helped Bush win re-election, and prominent Democrats were calling for a friendlier attitude toward religion and a bigger tent on social issues.

That was a long eight years ago. Since then, the sex abuse scandals that shadowed John Paul's last years have become the defining story of his successor's papacy, and the unexpected abdication of Benedict XVI has only confirmed the narrative of a church in disarray. His predecessor was buried amid reverent coverage from secular outlets, but the current pope can expect a send-off marked by sourness and shrugs.

The collapse in the church's reputation has coincided with a substantial loss of Catholic influence in American political debates. Whereas eight years ago, a Catholic view of economics and culture represented a center that both parties hoped to claim, today's Republicans are more likely to channel Ayn Rand than Thomas Aquinas, and a strident social liberalism holds the whip hand in the Democratic Party.

Indeed, between Mitt Romney's comments about the mooching 47 percent and the White House's cynical decision to energize its base by picking fights over abortion and contraception, both parties spent 2012 effectively running against Catholic ideas about the common good.

This transformation suggests that we may have reached the end of a distinctive "Catholic moment" (to repurpose a phrase from the late Catholic priest-intellectual Richard John Neuhaus) in American politics, one that began in the 1980s after John Paul's ascension to the papacy and the migration of many Catholic "Reagan Democrats" into the Republican Party.

This was hardly the first era when Catholic ideas shaped American debates. (New Deal-era liberalism, for instance, owed a major debt to Catholic social thought.) But it was the first era when the Catholic vote was both frequently decisive and genuinely up for grabs, and it was an era when Catholic debates and personalities filled the vacuum left by the decline of the Protestant mainline.

The fact that the Second Vatican Council had left the church internally divided limited Catholic influence in some ways but magnified it in others. Because the church's divisions often mirrored the country's, a politician who captured the typical Catholic voter was probably well on his way to victory, and so would-be leaders of both parties had every incentive to frame their positions in Catholic-friendly terms. The church might not always be speaking with one voice, but both left and right tried to borrow its language.

If this era is now passing, and Catholic ideas are becoming more marginal to our politics, it's partially because institutional Christianity is weaker over all than a generation ago, and partially because Catholicism's leaders have done their part, and then some, to hasten that de-Christianization. Any church that presides over a huge cover-up of sex abuse can hardly complain when its worldview is regarded with suspicion. The present pope has too often been scapegoated for the sex abuse crisis, but America's bishops have if anything gotten off too easily, and even now seem insufficiently chastened for their sins.

The recent turn away from Catholic ideas has also been furthered by a political class that never particularly cared for them in the first place. Even in a more unchurched America, a synthesis of social conservatism and more egalitarian-minded economic policies could have a great deal of mass appeal. But our elites seem mostly relieved to stop paying lip service to the Catholic synthesis: professional Republicans are more libertarian than their constituents, professional Democrats are more secular than their party's rank-and-file, and professional centrists get their encyclicals from Michael Bloomberg rather than the Vatican.

Nothing that happens in Rome over the next few months is likely to convert the Acela Corridor's donors and strategists and think tankers to a more Catholic-friendly worldview. The next pope may be more effective than Benedict, or he may be clumsier; he may improve the church's image in this country, or he may worsen it.

But if there is another Catholic moment waiting in our nation's future, it can only be made by Americans themselves.

ROSS DOUTHAT is an Op-Ed columnist for The New York Times.

Cardinals Start to Ponder Subtleties of a Big Task

BY DANIEL J. WAKIN | MARCH 4, 2013

VATICAN CITY — Like first-year seminarians, they walked through the glass doors on Monday carrying briefcases. Some arrived in chauffeured cars and taxis. Wearing long black coats and red caps, they took their assigned places in maroon lecture-halls seats, flipped through the assigned reading, recited prayers and swore on the Bible to "maintain rigorous secrecy" about their task.

Some 145 cardinals gathered on the first day of meetings required upon the end of a papacy — usually by death, but in this rare case, resignation. The morning session was devoted to preparatory matters. Through the week, the cardinals will discuss matters of importance to the church and choose a date — possibly as early as Sunday or Monday — for the conclave to elect a successor to Benedict XVI, who stepped aside last week.

The general congregation, as it is called, will also be a chance for the cardinals to make a case for what kind of pope they want, and to size one another up at coffee breaks and later over dinner. All have emphasized in interviews over the past week that they want a prayerful pope who can effectively transmit the Catholic message.

But nuances are already emerging. Some say they want a pope capable of reforming the bureaucracy of the Vatican, which has been hit with accusations of corruption in the past year. Others suggest a pope must come from the Third World, where Roman Catholicism is more vibrant than Europe. Still others want a pope with a strong governing hand.

On Monday, a senior American cardinal made a rare mention of the clerical sexual abuse scandal in that discourse. Cardinal Francis George, the archbishop of Chicago, said the new pope "obviously has to accept the universal code of the church now, which is zero tolerance for anyone who has abused a child." Speaking in answer to a question at a news conference, Cardinal George said, "There's a deep-seated conviction, certainly on the part of anyone who has been a pastor, that this has to be continually addressed."

The cardinal asserted that efforts by American churchmen had led to a sharp reduction in reported abuse cases. "But there's still the victims," he continued. "The wound is still deep in their hearts, and as long as it's with them it will be with us. The pope has to keep this in mind."

The church's response to the latest wave of sexual abuse scandals, which emerged with full force a decade ago in the United States and in Europe and elsewhere more recently, has not been the subject of as much discussion in the lead-up to the conclave. But it was not surprising that an American prelate addressed the matter so forcefully. In 2002, United States bishops pressed a "zero tolerance" policy — the rapid removal from ministry of any priest credibly accused of abuse — and other nations' bishops followed suit in later years. The Vatican has also taken a number of steps that it says will tighten sanctions against abuser priests.

One advocate for clerical abuse victims, David Clohessy of the Survivors Network of Those Abused by Priests, called Cardinal George's statement encouraging. "It should be a topic and we are glad that Cardinal George said it will be and must be," he said, "but the focus has got to be on safeguarding kids first, healing victims second."

Separately, Vatican officials declined to comment on the acknowledgment on Sunday by Cardinal Keith O'Brien, the most senior Roman Catholic cleric in Britain and a vehement condemner of homosexuality, that he had engaged in inappropriate sexual conduct. He announced his resignation a week earlier and said he was not coming to the conclave after three priests and a former priest accused him of making improper advances decades ago.

Questions may arise among the cardinals, Cardinal George suggested, about a report by three senior cardinals on corruption and leaks within the Vatican bureaucracy, or Curia, that was ordered by Benedict. Benedict consigned the report to his successor, and it remains secret.

Inside the Conclave

The last few conclaves have been brief, with the selection of a pope in just a few days. In 2005, Pope Benedict XVI was elected a day after the conclave began.

Cardinals stay at Santa Marta residence, less than a quarter-mile from the Sistine Chapel, where the voting happens.

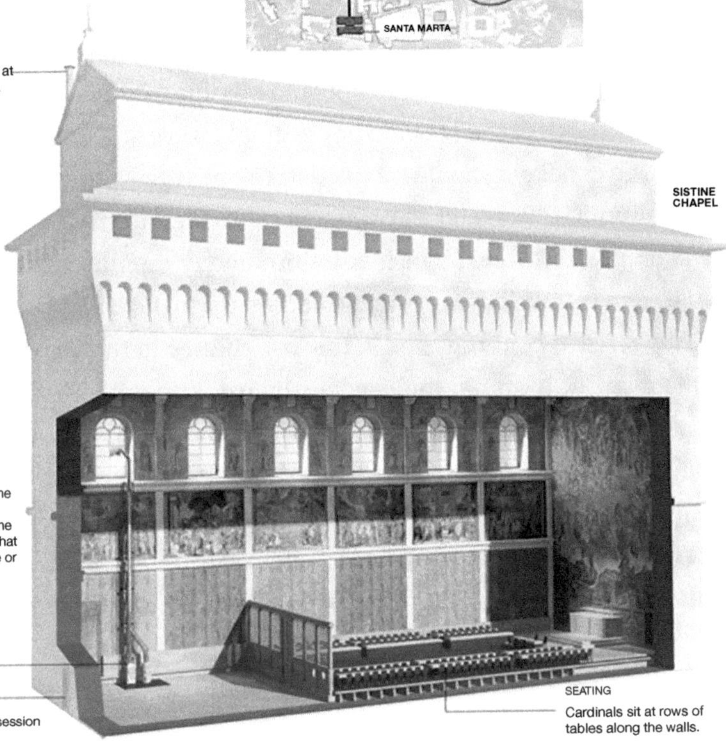

THE VOTING

Cardinals write a name under the Latin words "Eligo in Summum Pontificem" (I elect as Supreme Pontiff) and place the ballot in an urn.

Two cardinals read the ballot and record it. A third reads it aloud. The ballots are then threaded together through the word "Eligo."

Three cardinals check the ballots. If a candidate has received a two-thirds majority, then a new pope has been elected.

The cardinals burn the ballots, usually combining papers from two rounds of voting. Chemicals are added to make the smoke white if a pope has been elected, and black if not.

When a selection is made, the new pope chooses his papal name. Minutes later, he greets the world from the balcony of St. Peter's.

THE NEW YORK TIMES

Bathed in mystery and, many believe, the Holy Spirit, the conclave to elect a new pope marries the highest Catholic Church solemnity with one of history's longest-lived electoral experiences.

"I imagine that as we move along, there will be questioning of the cardinals involved in the governing of the Curia to see what they think has to be changed," he said. "Anything can come up."

The cardinals met in the Paul VI hall, a building where popes normally hold general audiences and where bishops from around the world gather in synods. No date for the conclave's start can be set until all the elector cardinals — those under 80 and eligible to vote — arrive. Father Lombardi said 8 of the 115 elector cardinals were still on their way. The date of the conclave should be fixed in the next few days, he said.

Cardinal George said the eminences wanted to have a pope before the start of Holy Week, which is Palm Sunday on March 24, but would not be rushed. "We'll take the time necessary to do the job well," he said.

The general congregation is the last chance in this process for cardinals over 80 to make their voices heard, and while time limits are imposed on speakers, the older crowd is indulged, past participants have said. Thirty-nine over-age cardinals were present on Monday, Father Lombardi said. The college has 207 members over all.

The Vatican press operation appears to be making an effort to be more open about what is by definition a highly secretive process. Telepace, an Italian-based Catholic television station, showed the cardinals going into the hall live. The Vatican has promised daily news conferences.

"Perhaps they decided that it's best to talk to the press rather than not talk to the press," Cardinal George said.

At the Vatican news conference, reporters were shown clips of the prelates inside the hall, walking past heavily draped windows in a corridor, entering the assembly hall and taking their seats in the raked auditorium, chatting with each other and flipping through the book of conclave ritual with its green hard cover, the Ordo rituum conclavis.

The cardinals sat in assigned seats to make it easier to keep attendance and keep track of who speaks, Father Lombardi said.

The princes of the church will speak through a microphone, which at the last conclave, in 2005, would be cut off generally after roughly seven minutes, Cardinal George said in an interview. Interpreters, sworn to secrecy, will render their comments into English, Spanish, Italian, German and French.

The cardinals agreed to send a message to Benedict, who has retreated to the papal summer home in Castel Gandolfo outside of Rome. Much of the session, which began at 9:30 a.m., was taken up with each man walking to the front table for the personal oath. At 11 a.m., they took a half-hour break, holding cardinal kaffeeklatsches. "It was an important moment for personal contacts, for exchanges at a more particular level," Father Lombardi said.

A baker's dozen of eminences spoke during a brief session, but mainly about logistical matters.

"As a start, it was very positive," Father Lombardi said.

Cardinals Pick Bergoglio, Who Will Be Pope Francis

BY RACHEL DONADIO | MARCH 13, 2013

VATICAN CITY — With a puff of white smoke from the chimney of the Sistine Chapel and to the cheers of thousands of rain-soaked faithful, a gathering of Catholic cardinals picked a new pope from among their midst on Wednesday — choosing the cardinal from Argentina, the first South American to lead the church.

The new pope, Jorge Mario Bergoglio (pronounced Ber-GOAL-io), will be called Francis, the 266th pontiff of the Roman Catholic Church. He is also the first non-European pope in more than 1,200 years and the first member of the Jesuit order to lead the church.

In choosing Francis, 76, who had been the archbishop of Buenos Aires, the cardinals sent a powerful message that the future of the church lies in the global south, home to the bulk of the world's Catholics.

"I would like to thank you for your embrace," the new pope, dressed in white, said from the white balcony on St. Peter's Basilica as thousands cheered joyously below. "My brother cardinals have chosen one who is from far away, but here I am."

Speaking in Italian as he blessed the faithful, Francis asked the audience to "pray for me, and we'll see each other soon."

"Good night, and have a good rest," he concluded, in a grandfatherly, almost casual tone.

"Habemus papam!" members of the crowd shouted in Latin, waving umbrellas and flags. "We have a pope!" Others cried, "Viva il Papa!"

"It was like waiting for the birth of a baby, only better," said a Roman man, Giuliano Uncini. A child sitting atop his father's shoulders waved a crucifix.

Francis is known as a humble man who spoke out for the poor and led an austere life in Buenos Aires. He was born to Italian immigrant parents and was raised in the Argentine capital.

The new pope inherits a church wrestling with an array of challenges that intensified during his predecessor, Benedict XVI, including a shortage of priests, growing competition from evangelical churches in the Southern Hemisphere, a sexual abuse crisis that has undermined the church's moral authority in the West and difficulties governing the Vatican itself.

Benedict abruptly ended his troubled eight-year papacy last month, announcing he was no longer up to the rigors of the job. He became the first pontiff in 598 years to resign. The 115 cardinals who are younger than 80 and eligible to vote chose their new leader after two days of voting.

Pope Francis spoke by telephone with Benedict on Wednesday evening, said a Vatican spokesman, the Rev. Federico Lombardi. He called it "an act of great significance and pastorality" that Francis' first act as pope was to offer a prayer for his predecessor.

The Rev. Thomas Rosica of Canada, another Vatican spokesman, recalled meeting Cardinal Bergoglio a decade ago during preparations for World Youth Day in Canada, and said the cardinal had told him that he lived very simply, in an apartment Buenos Aires, and sold the archdiocese's mansion.

"He cooks for himself and took great pride in telling us that, and that he took the bus to work" rather than riding in a car, Father Rosica said.

President Obama was among the first world leaders to congratulate Francis in a message that emphasized the pope's humble roots and New World background.

"As a champion of the poor and the most vulnerable among us, he carries forth the message of love and compassion that has inspired the world for more than 2,000 years — that in each other we see the face of God," Mr. Obama said in a message released by the White House.

"As the first pope from the Americas," the president added, "his selection also speaks to the strength and vitality of a region that is increasingly shaping our world, and alongside millions of Hispanic Americans, those of us in the United States share the joy of this historic day."

MAURICIO LIMA/THE NEW YORK TIMES

People pray during mass at the Metropolitan Cathedral in Buenos Aires, Argentina, in March 2013. At the formal start of his papacy, Pope Francis offered a passionate pledge to serve.

A doctrinal conservative, Francis has opposed liberation theology, abortion, gay marriage and the ordination of women, standing with his predecessor in holding largely traditional views.

As archbishop of Buenos Aires beginning in 1998 and a cardinal since 2001, he frequently tangled with Argentina's governments over social issues. In 2010, for example, he castigated a government-supported law to legalize marriage and adoption by same-sex couples as "a war against God."

He has been less energetic, however, in urging the Argentine church to examine its own behavior during the 1970s, when the country was consumed by a conflict between right and left. In what became known as the Dirty War, as many as 30,000 people were disappeared, tortured or killed by a military dictatorship that seized power in March 1976.

In a long interview with an Argentine newspaper in 2010, Cardinal

Bergoglio defended his behavior during the dictatorship. He said that he had helped hide people being sought for arrest or disappearance by the military because of their political views, had helped others leave Argentina and had lobbied the country's military rulers directly for the release and protection of others.

Before beginning the voting by secret ballot in the Sistine Chapel on Tuesday, in a cloistered meeting known as a conclave, the cardinals swore an oath of secrecy in Latin, a rite designed to protect deliberations from outside scrutiny — and to protect cardinals from earthly influence as they seek divine guidance.

The conclave followed more than a week of intense, broader discussions among the world's cardinals about the problems facing the church and their criteria for its next leader.

"We spoke among ourselves in an exceptional and free way, with great truth, about the lights but also about shadows in the current situation of the Catholic Church," Cardinal Christoph Schönborn of Vienna, a theologian known for his intellect and his pastoral touch, told reporters this week.

"The pope's election is something substantially different from a political election," Cardinal Schönborn said, adding that the role was not "the chief executive of a multinational company, but the spiritual head of a community of believers."

Indeed, Benedict was selected in 2005 as a caretaker after the momentous papacy of John Paul II, but the shy theologian appeared to show little inclination toward management. His papacy suffered from crises of communications — with Muslims, Jews and Anglicans — that, along with a sex abuse crisis that raged back to life in Europe in 2010, evolved into a crisis of governance.

Critics of Benedict's secretary of state, Cardinal Tarcisio Bertone, said he had difficulties in running the Vatican and appeared more interested in the Vatican's ties to Italy than to the rest of the world. The Vatican is deeply concerned about the fate of Christians in the war-torn Middle East.

The new pope will also inherit power struggles over the management of the Vatican bank, which must continue a process of meeting international transparency standards or risk being shut out of the mainstream international banking system. In one of his final acts as pope, Benedict appointed a German aristocrat, Ernst von Freyberg, as the bank's new president.

Francis will have to help make the Vatican bureaucracy — often seen as a hornet's nest of infighting Italians — work more efficiently for the good of the church. After years in which Benedict and John Paul helped consolidate more power at the top, many liberal Catholics also hope that the new pope will give local bishops' conferences more decision-making power to help respond to the needs of the faithful.

The reform of the Roman Curia, which runs the Vatican, "is not conceptually hard," said Alberto Melloni, the author of numerous books on the Vatican and the Second Vatican Council. "It's hard on a political front, but it will take five minutes for someone who has the strength. You get rid of the spoil system, and that's it."

The hard things are "if you want a permanent consultation of bishops' conferences," he added.

For Mr. Melloni, foreign policy and the church's vision of Asia would be crucial to the new pope. "If Roman Catholicism was capable of learning Greek while it was speaking Aramaic, of learning Celtic while it was speaking Latin, now it either has to learn Chinese or 'ciao,' " he said, using the Italian world for "goodbye."

Ahead of the election, cardinals said they were looking for "a pope that understands the problems of the church at present" and who is strong enough to tackle them, said Cardinal Miloslav Vlk, the archbishop emeritus of Prague, who participated in the general congregations but was not eligible to vote in a conclave.

He said those problems included reforming the Roman Curia, handling the sex abuse crisis and cleaning up the Vatican bank.

"He needs to be capable of solving these issues," Cardinal Vlk said as he walked near the Vatican this week, adding that the next pope needs "to be open to the world, to the troubles of the world, to society, because evangelization is a primary task, to bring the Gospel to people."

The sexual abuse crisis remains a troubling issue for the church, especially in English-speaking countries where victims sued dioceses found to have moved around abusive priests.

On Wednesday, news reports in California showed that one cardinal elector, Cardinal Roger M. Mahony, the former archbishop of Los Angeles; the archdiocese; and a former priest had reached a settlement of almost $10 million in four child sex abuse cases, according to the victims' lawyers.

Becoming pope also has a human dimension. In one of his final speeches as pope before he retired on Feb. 18, Benedict said his successor would need to be prepared to lose some of his privacy.

Reporting was contributed by **DANIEL J. WAKIN**, **LAURIE GOODSTEIN**, **STEFANIA ROUSSELLE** and **GAIA PIANIGIANI** from Vatican City, **ALAN COWELL** from Paris, **LARRY ROHTER** from Portland, Ore., and **RICK GLADSTONE** from New York.

A Conservative With a Common Touch

BY EMILY SCHMALL AND LARRY ROHTER | MARCH 13, 2013

BUENOS AIRES — Like most of those in Argentina, he is a soccer fan, his favorite team being the underdog San Lorenzo squad. Known for his outreach to the country's poor, he gave up a palace for a small apartment, rode public transportation instead of a chauffeur-driven car and cooked his own meals.

The new pope, Jorge Mario Bergoglio (pronounced ber-GOAL-io), 76, will be called Francis. Chosen Wednesday by a gathering of Roman Catholic cardinals, he is in some ways a history-making pontiff, the first from the Jesuit order and the first pope from Latin America.

But Cardinal Bergoglio is also a conventional choice, a theological conservative of Italian ancestry who vigorously backs Vatican positions on abortion, gay marriage, the ordination of women and other major issues — leading to heated clashes with Argentina's left-leaning president.

He was less energetic, however, when it came to standing up to Argentina's military dictatorship during the 1970s as the country was consumed by a conflict between right and left that became known as the Dirty War. He has been accused of knowing about abuses and failing to do enough to stop them, during a period when as many as 30,000 people were abducted, tortured or killed by the dictatorship.

Despite the criticism, many here praise Cardinal Bergoglio — who likes the more humble title of Father Jorge — as a passionate defender of the poor and disenfranchised.

In 2001 he surprised the staff of Muñiz Hospital in Buenos Aires, asking for a jar of water, which he used to wash the feet of 12 patients hospitalized with complications from the virus that causes AIDS. He then kissed their feet, telling reporters that "society forgets the sick and the poor." More recently, in September 2012, he scolded priests in Buenos Aires who refused to baptize the children of unwed mothers.

“No to hypocrisy,” he said of the priests at the time. “They are the ones who separate the people of God from salvation.”

Though he is averse to liberation theology, which he views as hopelessly tainted with Marxist ideology, Cardinal Bergoglio has emphasized outreach to the impoverished, and as cardinal of Buenos Aires he has overseen increased social services and evangelization in the slums.

“I am encouraged by this choice, viewing it as a pledge for a church of simplicity and of ecological ideals,” said Leonardo Boff, a founder of liberation theology. What is more, Mr. Boff said, Cardinal Bergoglio comes from the developing world, “outside the walls of Rome.”

Jorge Mario Bergoglio was born in Buenos Aires on Dec. 17, 1936, to Mario Bergoglio, an immigrant from northern Italy, and Regina Bergoglio, a homemaker. He came relatively late to the priesthood, enrolling in a seminary only at the age of 21, after studying chemistry. He has had health concerns since his youth, having had a lung removed because of an infection.

By all accounts, he was a brilliant student who relished the study not just of theology but also of secular subjects like psychology and literature. He was ordained a priest a few days short of turning 33, and from that point on, his ascent within the church was rapid: by 1973, he had been named the Jesuit provincial for Argentina, the church official in charge of supervising the order’s activities in the country.

He remained in that post through 1979, and his performance during the Dirty War has been the subject of controversy. In 2005, shortly before the Vatican conclave that elevated Cardinal Joseph Ratzinger to the papacy, Cardinal Bergoglio was formally accused by an Argentine lawyer in a lawsuit of being complicit in the military’s kidnapping of two Jesuit priests whose antigovernment views he considered dangerously unorthodox.

The priests, whom he had dismissed from the order a week before they disappeared, were discovered months later on the outskirts of Buenos Aires, drugged and partially undressed. At the time the lawsuit was filed, the cardinal’s spokesman dismissed the accusations as “old slander.”

The lawsuit was eventually dismissed, but the debate has continued, with Argentine journalists publishing articles and books that appear to contradict Cardinal Bergoglio's account of his actions. These accounts draw not only on documents from the period, but also on statements by priests and lay workers who clashed with Cardinal Bergoglio.

After the church had denied for years any involvement with the dictatorship, he testified in 2010 that he had met secretly with Gen. Jorge Videla, the former head of the military junta, and Adm. Emilio Massera, the commander of the navy, to ask for the release of the priests. The following year, prosecutors called him to the witness stand to testify on the military junta's systematic kidnapping of children, a subject he was also accused of knowing about but failing to prevent.

In a long interview published by an Argentine newspaper in 2010, he defended his behavior during the dictatorship. He said that he had helped hide people being sought for arrest or disappearance by the military because of their political views, had helped others leave Argentina and had lobbied the country's military rulers directly for the release and protection of others.

In November 2005, Cardinal Bergoglio was elected head of the Argentine Conference of Bishops for a three-year term, which was renewed in 2008. At the time he was chosen, the Argentine church was dealing with a notorious political scandal, that of the Rev. Christian von Wernich, a former chaplain of the Buenos Aires police who had been accused of aiding in the questioning, torture and death of political prisoners.

The church authorities had spirited Father von Wernich out of the country and placed him in a parish in Chile under a false name, but he was eventually brought back to Argentina and put on trial. In 2007, he was found guilty on seven counts of complicity in homicide, more than 40 counts of kidnapping and more than 30 of torture, and was sentenced to life imprisonment.

Father von Wernich was allowed to continue to celebrate Mass in prison, and in 2010 a church official said that "at the appropriate time, von Wernich's situation will have to be resolved in accordance with canonical law." But Cardinal Bergoglio never issued a formal apology on behalf of the church, or commented directly on the case, and during his tenure the bishops' conference was similarly silent.

Only in November 2012, a year after Cardinal Bergoglio had stepped down as head of the bishops' conference, did the group address the issue of its role during the dictatorship. It came in response to remarks in which the former dictator, General Videla, had, in the words of the statement the bishops issued, "attributed to those who then led the Conference complicity in criminal acts." The bishops' statement denied General Videla's accusation and claimed that church leaders of the time "tried to do what was within their reach for the welfare of all."

Asked Wednesday about Cardinal Bergoglio's role during the Dirty War, the archbishop of Washington, Cardinal Donald Wuerl, said, "I haven't seen anything other than conjecture."

In recent years, Cardinal Bergoglio has clashed with the Argentine government, particularly former President Néstor Kirchner and his successor and widow, Cristina Fernández de Kirchner, about issues like gay marriage, abortion and the adoption of children by gay couples. In 2010, he described a government-supported law to legalize marriage and adoption by same-sex couples as "a war against God" and "a maneuver by the devil."

At the time, Mrs. Kirchner said, "Bergoglio's position is medieval." But on Wednesday, after he was announced as the new pope, she appeared willing to smooth over their differences, congratulating him and telling him he had her "consideration and respect."

Horacio Verbitsky, an Argentine journalist who has investigated claims of ties between Cardinal Bergoglio and Argentina's military rulers, said he expected the new pope to be "extremely conservative in all doctrinaire questions, yet open to the world and, above all, to the world of the poor."

EMILY SCHMALL reported from Buenos Aires, and **LARRY ROHTER** from Portland, Ore. **SIMON ROMERO** contributed reporting from Rio de Janeiro, and **MAURICIO RABUFFETTI** from Montevideo, Uruguay.

Life on the Papal Beat

BY RACHEL DONADIO | SEPT. 18, 2015

IN THE TWO SHORT YEARS since his election, Pope Francis has managed an unusual feat: He has become as beloved by the international news media and the secular intelligentsia as by his own flock of 1.2 billion. I got a taste of what has been called "the Francis effect" when, on a sweltering July day, I watched dozens of mayors from around the world gather at the Vatican for a two-day conference on climate change.

Just weeks before, Francis' encyclical on the environment, "Laudato Si," had landed with an impact rarely seen from a 40,000-word papal document. The New York Times and other news outlets covered the encyclical as a developing story, posting continual updates online as reactions poured in from environmentalists, from industrialists and from the faithful around the world. The conference had been hastily organized by the Pontifical Academies of Sciences and Social Sciences and Jeffrey Sachs, the prominent economist and director of the Sustainable Development Solutions Network. Such a collaboration would have been rare in the past but represents the kind of bridge Francis is building between the church and the wider world.

The conference was being held in a small amphitheater upstairs from the 1970s-era Paul VI audience hall, just to the left of St. Peter's Basilica. There was more security than usual — two sets of metal detectors — most likely because of the visiting politicians. (The Vatican tries not to put barriers between the faithful and the pope.) Inside the auditorium, a few dozen journalists had gathered: veteran reporters and photographers for wire services, some of whom had spent decades covering the Vatican. I chatted with an Argentine journalist for a Latin American news wire. His star had risen with the new Argentine pope, who has drawn many new arrivals from Latin America into the Vatican press corps. This influx has made getting a coveted seat on the papal plane even more difficult. Competition was especially fierce for the pope's imminent trip to Cuba and the United States, not least because of his role in facilitating a private meeting at the Vatican last year between American and Cuban officials, which helped finalize the detente between the two countries. For the first time, some regular Italian outlets didn't get spots. Francis would not be addressing the press that day — popes never give news conferences and don't take questions in public; the only time they speak directly to the press corps is on the papal plane. Reporters were there mainly to document the politicians eager to be in his orbit.

Francis finally appeared at the end of the day, with little fanfare and without an entourage. As people applauded and began filming him with their phones, the pope took his seat. He wore a simple cross over his white robe. He seemed a bit fatigued — temperatures were nearly 100 degrees — but he spoke off the cuff in Spanish for a long while. He warned of "the idolatry of technocracy," which he said leads to unemployment. He spoke of the exploitation of children, of migration and the risks of deforestation, especially in the Amazon, which he called one of the "great lungs" of the world. He told the mayors he was very glad they had traveled to the Vatican to discuss environmental issues, because change has to start from the grass roots. "The most serious and profound work," he concluded, "starts at the peripheries and moves toward the center."

I hadn't been back to the Vatican in two years, and it was immediately clear how much had changed. When I covered the Vatican as the Rome bureau chief for The New York Times, from 2008 to 2013, conferences and encyclicals were generally not seen as developing stories. My tenure began three years into the troubled papacy of Benedict XVI, a conservative German theologian ill at ease with his public persona, whose most transformative act may have been his surprise resignation. He spoke often about "logos," which can mean "reason," and how to reconcile it with faith, and he seemed most preoccupied by encroaching secularism, not pressing global issues like climate change. Benedict, with his careful shuffle of a walk, his tremulous voice, his insistence on intellectual rigor in Catholic practice, seemed to suggest that the church might just have lost the culture wars. Francis, whose folksy joviality deflects attention from his sharp political instincts, presents the church as fully engaged in a battle that there may still be a chance of winning — for souls, yes, but also for the planet.

In 2008, on my way to the Vatican press office for my first meeting, I stopped in St. Peter's Square. Part of the square is an ellipse designed by Bernini, the master of the Italian Baroque. From most points, the colonnade's four rows of thick columns are visible, but at a precise spot on either side, they align and fuse into one. In the years to come, I would think often of that spot as key to so much about the Vatican, this ancient institution built of solid stone and optical illusion, where perspective is all. You cannot understand the Vatican without understanding the Baroque — a movement that relied not only on complexity for complexity's sake but also on trompe l'oeil and perspectival techniques to represent multiple angles of vision simultaneously. And you cannot understand, or govern, Italy without understanding the Vatican, whose most abiding lesson is: Time is power.

How else to make sense of the endless and elaborate delays, the delicate art of manipulating the interlocking gears of the machine, the tug of war between Rome and the local dioceses — all of which produces a perpetual displacement of responsibility that often erodes the line between willful obfuscation and benign incompetence. What providence wills, only bureaucracy can achieve. He who slows down time preserves power. I once asked Giulio Andreotti, the seven-time Christian Democratic prime minister of Italy, the enigmatic force at the center of so many webs who never so much as flinched during the years of trials for associating with the Mafia — in which he was, naturally, acquitted — why Italy was so bureaucratic. "It's a certain guarantee," Andreotti answered, sitting in his Senate office and speaking in his clipped monotone, his shoulders slightly hunched. "Yes, it's a weight, maybe something flat and opaque, but it's also a guarantee to go one step at a time, not to take big curves. If you take big curves fast, that can be very risky."

At the Vatican, the Apostolic Palace is the seat of power. Francis

answer a yes-or-no question — he preferred the formulation that something was "a cammino," "a path," and I often wondered where, precisely, we might be on the journey and what we might see at the end of it. In 2010, in the middle of the clergy sexual-abuse crisis, I sent Lombardi a question about how the Vatican had handled the case of an abusive priest in Chile. Lombardi responded that appropriate measures had been taken at the appropriate time. I sent a follow-up question, the gist of which was "Who knew what when?" His answer came back: "Respondit eis Pilatus: 'Quod scripsi, scripsi.'" "Pilate said to him: 'What I have written, I have written.'" (The Gospel of John: 19:22.)

In July, I stopped by to see Lombardi for the first time in a few years. He greeted me warmly with the informal "tu," while I, as was our habit, used the formal "Lei." I sat on a worn leather sofa and he on a swivel chair. He was in good spirits. Francis' trip to Latin America in June had gone very well. The encyclical on the environment, he said, had already become a best seller in some countries. Excitement was building for the pope's trip to the United States and Cuba. I asked him if it was challenging to keep up with Francis, who improvises constantly. He rolled his eyes. "Don't even tell me about it," he said. There was no nervous cough.

Under Benedict, Lombardi was forever trying to prevent the fallout from a crisis. Under Francis, his repeated message seems to be that the pope, in spite of his focus on those on the margins of society, is not, in fact, a Marxist. He mentioned the pope's speech in Bolivia, in which Francis spoke of the periphery as a catalyst of creativity and moral engagement. The speech "could be read as leftist revolutionary, because it largely makes an appeal to the poor," Lombardi said. "But there was not a single word about class warfare. There's not a single word about violence. It's all about common good and love and responsibility."

It falls on Lombardi to make clear that both popes speak for the same church. And it falls on the press to describe what we see. Four rows of columns or one? As always, it's a question of perspective.

RACHEL DONADIO is the European culture correspondent for The New York Times and is based in Paris. She was The Times's Rome bureau chief from 2008 to 2013.

CHAPTER 2

The Pope's Theological and Social Teachings

Popes command significant authority in the spiritual teachings of Catholicism. Francis' theological writings have sparked intense public debate. In his encyclicals and less authoritative apostolic exhortations, Francis' writings have relaxed earlier church doctrine on sexual morality to highlight questions of social justice and ecology. Francis' most controversial exhortation, "Amoris Laetitia," drew ire from conservatives for moderating the Church's traditional stance on homosexuality and divorce. Francis also loosened restrictions on translating Catholic liturgy.

Pope Sets Down Goals for an Inclusive Church, Reaching Out 'on the Streets'

BY LAURIE GOODSTEIN AND ELISABETTA POVOLEDO | NOV. 26, 2013

IN HIS FIRST nine months as leader of one billion Roman Catholics, Pope Francis has parceled out glimpses of his vision for remaking the church in homilies and news conferences, interviews and offhand remarks to visitors.

On Tuesday, he announced his agenda in his own unfiltered words, reaffirming the impression that he intends to jolt the church out of complacency and enlist all Catholics in his ambitious project of renewing the church by confronting the real needs of people in need.

In a challenge to the Vatican hierarchy, Francis called for decentralizing power in the church, saying the Vatican and even the pope must collaborate with bishops, laypeople and in particular women.

"I prefer a church which is bruised, hurting and dirty because it has been out on the streets, rather than a church which is unhealthy from being confined and from clinging to its own security," Francis said in the first teaching document of his papacy that he alone composed.

"I do not want a church concerned with being at the center and then ends by being caught up in a web of obsessions and procedures," he wrote.

The document, called "Evangelii Gaudium" (the Joy of the Gospel), is an apostolic exhortation — less authoritative than an encyclical, but an important pronouncement. He drafted it in August in Spanish, said a Vatican spokesman, the Rev. Federico Lombardi, as a reflection on a synod of bishops last year that took up the "new evangelization."

Francis' prescription for the church is inextricably tied up with his analysis of what is wrong with the world. He devotes many pages to denouncing the "dictatorship" of a global economic system and a free market that perpetuates inequality and "devours" what is fragile, including human beings and the environment.

"How can it be that it is not a news item when an elderly homeless person dies of exposure, but it is news when the stock market loses two points?" he wrote, in the folksy language that has already marked his as a memorable papacy.

Vincent J. Miller, a theologian who writes on economic globalization at the University of Dayton, a Catholic university, said that while other popes have critiqued the economy, Francis has perspective on economic injustice as the first pope from Latin America, and is putting forward the church as the counterpoint.

"He talks about an economy of exclusion, while he's been modeling and practicing inclusion publicly through his whole papacy," Mr. Miller said.

After months in which many have parsed his comments for hints of change, the pope used the document to reiterate church teachings on abortion, homosexuality and the ordination of women. On abortion, he said, "It is not 'progressive' to try to resolve problems by eliminating a human life. On the other hand, it is also true that we have done little to adequately accompany women in very difficult situations," who may seek abortions because of rape or extreme poverty.

Nowhere in the document did Francis speak explicitly of homosexuality or same-sex marriage. However, he said the church should not give in to "moral relativism," and cited with approval a document written by the bishops of the United States on ministering to people with "homosexual inclination." The pope said the American bishops are right that the church must insist on "objective moral norms which are valid for everyone," even when the church is perceived by supporters of gay rights as promoting prejudice and interfering with individual freedom.

Echoing his predecessors, Francis said that ordaining women to the priesthood "is not a question open to discussion." He acknowledged that "many women share pastoral responsibilities with priests," and said, "We need to create still broader opportunities for a more incisive female presence in the church." But he offered no specifics on doing so.

But the document dwells at length on how priests can preach better homilies, which he said are the "touchstone" for judging how close a pastor is with his people. Francis said that both clergy and laypeople suffer from homilies: "The laity from having to listen to them, and the clergy from having to preach them! It is sad that this is the case."

Francis criticized those within the church who foster division to the point of "veritable witch hunts." In recent years, some bishops in the United States and Europe have advocated denying the eucharist, or holy communion, to Catholic politicians who support abortion rights or same-sex marriage. Francis did not take up this issue directly, but he advocated open doors.

"Everyone can be part of the community, nor should the doors of the sacraments be closed for simply any reason," Francis said.

"The eucharist, although it is the fullness of sacramental life, is not a prize for the perfect but a powerful medicine and nourishment for the weak."

Francis proposed a vision of a decentralized church. Bishops and priests have a better sense of the needs of the faithful, he said. Parishes should be the point of "contact with the homes and the lives of its people," not a "useless structure out of touch with people or a self-absorbed cluster made up of a chosen few."

"Laypeople are, put simply, the vast majority of the people of God. The minority 'ordained ministers' are at their service," Francis wrote.

John Thavis, a former Vatican bureau chief for Catholic News Service, who wrote "The Vatican Diaries," said, "He's laying down some real markers about the kinds of reforms he expects to preside over, including greater decentralization, openness to diversity in the church, and a greater emphasis on the gospel message of salvation as opposed to church doctrines and rules."

The pope wrote that national bishops' conferences can be fruitful sounding boards.

Archbishop Lorenzo Baldisseri, secretary general of the Synod of Bishops, noted Tuesday that the document made repeated references to documents drafted by various bishops' conferences — a first. It signals the will "to allow the bishops of the world to participate in the leadership of the church," he said.

The Rev. Antonio Spadaro, editor of the leading Jesuit journal in Rome, who interviewed the pope last summer just as Francis was writing the exhortation, said, "It is an ample and profound document, which finds its roots in the pope's personal history."

"But it isn't complete," he said. "I think we'll see more."

LAURIE GOODSTEIN reported from New York, and **ELISABETTA POVOLEDO** from Rome.

Room for Debate: The New Pope's New Direction

OPINION | BY THE NEW YORK TIMES | NOV. 27, 2013

WHEN POPE FRANCIS issued an apostolic exhortation this week, he challenged the church on some issues but affirmed its positions on others: critiquing modern capitalism and the church's top-down hierarchy but agreeing that women should not be ordained.

What does Francis' exhortation tell us about his priorities and plans? What obstacles will he face?

POPE FRANCIS' CRITIQUE OF CAPITALISM

GARY DORRIEN, the Reinhold Niebuhr professor at Union Theological Seminary and a professor of religion at Columbia University, is the author, most recently, of "Kantian Reason and Hegelian Spirit: The Idealistic Logic of Modern Theology."

Pope Francis sent a strong message about the kind of pope that he wanted to be when he took his name. Any pope would have to be daring to evoke the memory of St. Francis of Assisi. Thus no pope had ever done it. Francis of Assisi famously embraced a spirit of radical simplicity after spurning the riches and advantages of a privileged background. Pope Francis, thus far, conveys a similar spirit, calling the church to a "bruised, hurting and dirty" life in the streets instead of protecting its material interests and security.

It remains to be seen whether Francis will press this way-of-Christ theme beyond token gestures. Catholic Worker communities and religious orders that minister to the poor and excluded have long done so, and it will be fitting if the church confers sainthood on the Catholic Worker founder, Dorothy Day, during Francis' papacy. If, however, Francis pursues his attack on the "new tyranny" of unfettered capitalism, he will need to draw upon and renew a deeper well of teaching about political economy — the 122-year tradition of modern Catholic social thought, in which the key figure is a more worldly thinker, Pope Leo XIII.

In the 1891 encyclical Rerum Novarum, Leo XIII pioneered the Catholic tradition of protesting that under capitalism "a small number of very rich men have been able to lay upon the teeming masses of the laboring poor a yoke little better than that of slavery itself." According to Leo, the capitalist system was defined by "the callousness of employers and the greed of unrestrained competition," including its drive to leave workers "isolated and defenseless." The existing capitalist system was morally repugnant because it released individuals from their moral and social obligations. Socialism, on the other hand, was an overreaction to capitalism that violated the spiritual nature and rights of individuals. Leo pleaded that there had to be a decent alternative to predatory economics and collectivist economics.

More than a century later, we are still in the early stages of discerning what that would be.

EXPECT MORE SURPRISES FROM POPE FRANCIS

COLLEEN CARROLL CAMPBELL, the executive producer and anchor of "EWTN News Nightly With Colleen Carroll Campbell," is the author, most recently, of "My Sisters the Saints: A Spiritual Memoir."

Francis is a pope of surprises, a plainspoken, warm-hearted shepherd who has a habit of afflicting the comfortable even as he comforts the afflicted. In his wide-ranging apostolic exhortation this week, he pulls no punches, calling committed Catholics and nonbelievers alike to a searching examination of conscience.

"The Joy of the Gospel" covers a vast amount of territory. Topics range from the pope's feisty critique of trickle-down economics to his re-affirmation of church teaching against abortion and his advice that long-winded priests learn from mothers of young children how to deliver homilies that are punchier and less pretentious. But the heart of the pope's message is precisely what the title suggests: A reminder of the Gospel imperative that Christians live their faith with contagious joy, remaining always open to the surprising promptings of the Holy Spirit.

The third person of the Trinity gets top billing in Francis' document. Again and again, the pope asks readers to reflect on how God's still, small voice might be speaking in their lives, inviting them to turn away from their idols of money, power, career or comfort and rediscover the joy that comes from generous service to others and to God. Like the patron saint from whom he took his papal name, Francis harbors a passion for the poor, impatience with the ecclesial status quo and a burning desire to reawaken his fellow Catholics to the riches of a life spent "fearlessly open to the working of the Holy Spirit."

The pope is pointed in his criticism of the tendency among Christians to take one aspect of the Gospel and run with it, to the exclusion of all others. Catholics who embrace the church's social justice advocacy but evince embarrassment about the living faith that animates that advocacy come in for critique. So, too, do Catholics who embrace the moral teachings and liturgical traditions but ignore the needs of the poor and wind up trapped in "a narcissistic and authoritarian elitism, whereby instead of evangelizing, one analyzes and classifies others."

Whether calling out the totalitarian impulse of strident secularists who would banish religion from the public square or lamenting today's chic, do-it-yourself spirituality that winds up imprisoning its practitioners in self-centeredness, Francis does not mince words. But even as the pope challenges readers with razor-sharp insights on some of the most intimate struggles of the human heart, he does not come off haughty or didactic. Perhaps that's because "The Joy of the Gospel" is threaded throughout with Francis' characteristic humility and copious reminders of God's merciful, redeeming love.

This is the pope who, when asked in a recent interview to describe himself, said simply: "I am a sinner." He is a pastor known for walking closely with his sheep, learning from them and listening to them. And as the pope notes near the end of his exhortation, the trials and uncertainty of the spiritual life are familiar to him. "Trust in the unseen can cause us to feel disoriented," Francis writes. "It is like being plunged into the deep and not knowing what we will find. I myself have frequently experienced this. Yet there is no greater freedom than that of allowing oneself to be guided by the Holy Spirit, renouncing the attempt to plan and control everything to the last detail, and instead letting him enlighten, guide and direct us, leading us wherever he wills."

If Francis has a plan or program for his pontificate, that's probably a clear summary. Following the lead of a pope so devoted to following the promptings of the Holy Spirit, Catholics can surely expect more surprises to come.

WHY WOULD POPE FRANCIS KEEP WOMEN OUT OF THE PRIESTHOOD?

ERIN SAIZ HANNA is the executive director of the Women's Ordination Conference, which works to ordain women as priests, deacons and bishops.

Like Pope Francis' humble, pastoral nature, much of his 84-page document, Evangelii Gaudium, will win over the hearts of many Catholics. In this exhortation, which lays a clear blueprint for his papacy, Pope Francis calls for reform of the curia and global economic justice. As I read the document, I found myself really rooting for Francis when he said: "How can it be that it is not a news item when an elderly homeless person dies of exposure, but it is news when the stock market loses two points?" Yes. This is what Jesus would say. This is being Catholic.

But where Francis lost me is on the role of women in the church, where once again women are seen as a separate entity and unworthy of priestly ordination. Pope Francis reiterated we're not even allowed to discuss the issue. In the document, Francis states, "The reservation of the priesthood to males, as a sign of Christ the Spouse who gives himself in the Eucharist, is not a question open to discussion, but it can prove especially divisive if sacramental power is too closely identified with power in general."

Where Francis misses the mark is suggesting that women are seeking ordination simply as means to gain power. While women's decision making and leadership is certainly vital, the fact of the matter is women are called by God to serve alongside their brother priests. For a pope who seems so in tune with the marginalized, how does he not see that women are weeping and yearning for justice in the church?

How can his sense of social justice not extend to the women of the church and their capacity for ordained ministry?

By including women as priests, the church would model Jesus' radical example of equality and solidarity with women. It would also have a powerful and positive impact on a world stunned by economic crisis and continually reeling from sexism, racism, homophobia and other forms of oppression.

As Pope Francis continues his papacy, I believe keeping the hearts of women engaged will serve as a real obstacle for him. While many of Pope Francis' calls for reform are inspiring, when it comes to the role of women in the church, he is just another enforcer of the stained glass ceiling.

POPE FRANCIS IS EMBRACING THE LEPER AND THE DOWNTRODDEN

SISTER NORA NASH is the director of corporate social responsibility of the Sisters of St. Francis of Philadelphia.

Like Francis of Assisi, Pope Francis seems to find meaning in reverence for all creation. I believe that Francis is imbued with a sense of the truth, beauty and goodness inherent in every creature. This internal sense is persuasive as he reaches across the globe to call all people to conversion.

And like Francis of Assisi, he has embraced the leper and the downtrodden. Compassion and humility seem to be defining characteristics of Pope Francis, and he wants no part of power, prestige and wealth. Rather he sees that the purpose of his ministry is to serve in imitation of Jesus Christ, embracing "evangelii gaudium" — the joy of the gospel. Pope Francis does not judge, but recognizes that he (and we) cannot shirk responsibility for a world community that is plagued with injustices, ecological problems and alienation.

Like Francis of Assisi, Pope Francis will have many obstacles, both internally and externally. But I believe that he is confident those obstacles will be temporary road blocks in a church that will, for the most part, embrace the new life that is evident in his vision.

Pope Francis' Call to Action Goes Beyond the Environment

OPINION | BY ROSS DOUTHAT | JUNE 20, 2015

IN POPE FRANCIS' sprawling new encyclical, "Laudato Si'," there are many mansions: A meditation on biblical ecology, a discussion of environmental policy, a critique of consumerism, even a reflection on the perils of social media.

What everyone wants to know, of course, is whether the pope takes sides in our most polarizing debate. And he clearly does. After this document, there's no doubting where Francis stands in the great argument of our time.

But I don't mean the argument between liberalism and conservatism. I mean the argument between dynamists and catastrophists.

Dynamists are people who see 21st-century modernity as a basically successful civilization advancing toward a future that's better than the past. They do not deny that problems exist, but they believe we can innovate our way through them while staying on an ever-richer, ever-more-liberated course.

Dynamists of the left tend to put their faith in technocratic government; dynamists of the right, in the genius of free markets. But both assume that modernity is a success story whose best days are ahead.

Catastrophists, on the other hand, see a global civilization that for all its achievements is becoming more atomized and balkanized, more morally bankrupt, more environmentally despoiled. What's more, they believe that *things cannot go on as they are*: That the trajectory we're on will end in crisis, disaster, dégringolade.

Like dynamists, catastrophists can be on the left or right, stressing different agents of our imminent demise. But they're united in believing that current arrangements are foredoomed, and that only a true revolution can save us.

This is Pope Francis' position, and the controlling theme of his encyclical. It includes, as many liberals hoped and certain conservatives feared, a call to action against climate change, which will no doubt cause Republicans to squirm during political campaigns to come.

But reading "Laudato Si' " *simply* as a case for taking climate change seriously misses the depth of its critique — which extends to the whole "technological paradigm" of our civilization, all the ways (economic and cultural) that we live now.

This is a document aligned with the scientific consensus on climate that excoriates the modern scientific mind-set as, in effect, a 500-year mistake. It's a document calling for global action, even a "new world political authority," that's drenched in frank contempt for the existing global leadership class. It's a document that urges a rapid move away from fossil fuels while explicitly criticizing the leading avenue for doing so — a cap and trade regime — as too "quick and easy," too compromised by greed and self-interest, to "allow for the radical change which present circumstances require."

And while it includes hopeful passages, the encyclical's most pungent lines are apocalyptic: "Doomsday predictions can no longer be met with irony or disdain. We may well be leaving to coming generations debris, desolation and filth."

This pungency is what really distinguishes "Laudato Si' " from prior papal documents.

Francis' predecessors attempted versions of his double pitch — urging Catholics to recognize environmental devastation as a manifestation of the individualism the church has long condemned, while inviting secular readers to consider religious alternatives to our present way of life. But its urgency, sweep, and apocalyptic flavor may make "Laudato Si' " more immediately influential, more likely to make both audiences think anew.

However, its catastrophism also leaves this pope more open to empirical criticism. For instance, he doesn't grapple sufficiently with evidence that the global poor have become steadily less poor under precisely the world system he decries — a reality that has complicated implications for environmentalism.

Nor are questions related to population growth successfully resolved. If resource constraints are really as severe as the pope implies, and technological solutions as limited in power, it isn't entirely clear how the planet can sustain the steadily-growing population the Catholic vision of marriage and fecundity implies. To credibly make the case that a billions-strong human race can keep having large families, you might need a more, well, dynamist view of the human future than this encyclical contains.

Finally, it's possible to believe that climate change is happening while doubting that it makes "the present world system ... certainly unsustainable," as the pope suggests. Perhaps we'll face a series of chronic but manageable problems instead; perhaps "radical change" can, in fact, be persistently postponed.

Indeed, perhaps our immediate future fits neither the dynamist nor the catastrophist framework.

We might have entered a kind of *stagnationist* position, a sustainable decadence, in which the issues Pope Francis identifies percolate without reaching a world-altering boil.

In that case, the deep critique our civilization deserves will have to be advanced without the threat of imminent destruction. The arguments in "Laudato Si' " will still resonate, but they will have to be structured around a different peril: Not a fear that the particular evils of our age can't last, but the fear that actually, they can.

ROSS DOUTHAT is an Op-Ed columnist for The New York Times.

How Pope Francis' 'Amoris Laetitia' Could Affect Families and the Church

BY LAURIE GOODSTEIN AND JIM YARDLEY | APRIL 7, 2016

IN WHAT COULD BE an important moment for his leadership of the Roman Catholic Church, Pope Francis is scheduled to issue a major document on Friday regarding family issues. It is titled "Amoris Laetitia," Latin for "The Joy of Love."

In the document, known as an apostolic exhortation, the pope could change church practice on thorny subjects like whether divorced Catholics who remarry without having obtained annulments can receive holy communion. He might address debates over same-sex relationships, cohabitation and polygamy, an issue in Africa. Or, he could sidestep such divisive topics and stick to broader philosophical statements.

HOW LONG DID THIS TAKE?

For the past two years, Francis has guided the church through a sweeping exercise of self-examination that some scholars have compared to the Second Vatican Council. Catholics around the world filled out detailed questionnaires about whether the church meets their families' needs. Bishops and other church officials spent two tumultuous meetings at the Vatican, known as synods, debating and arguing.

The broad topic was whether the Catholic Church should reposition itself, and how. Francis listened, prodded and sometimes steered the process, but he mostly kept his own counsel. Until now.

WHAT'S AT STAKE?

Having led Catholics into such delicate terrain, Francis has stirred hope and fear. Some religious conservatives warn he could destabilize the church and undermine Catholic doctrine. Some liberals, though, are hoping Francis will directly address same-sex marriage and contraception in a way that would make the church more responsive to today's realities.

"I'm sure he knew he would touch some nerves," said John Thavis, a longtime Vatican analyst and the author of "The Vatican Diaries." "He may not have appreciated how much opposition there could be."

But both sides might be disappointed.

Some who study Francis predict the apostolic exhortation will be a broad statement on universal problems affecting families, like poverty, migration, domestic violence, health care, youth unemployment and the neglect of children and the elderly. Francis' encyclical on the environment, "Laudato Si'," released in June, was an enormous study in connecting the dots, and experts are expecting a similar sweep in "Amoris Laetitia."

"This document is meant for Catholics all over the world, some of whom are in desperate straits because of poverty and war and other crises that make having a family life almost impossible," said the Rev. Thomas J. Reese, a senior analyst for the American newspaper The National Catholic Reporter. "This pope, his heart aches for these people who are so marginalized. I'm sure this document will address that."

SO WHAT'S ALL THE FUSS ABOUT?

Francis signaled early on that he wanted the church to re-examine its ministry to those who feel excluded, calling bishops to two synod meetings on the family, in 2014 and 2015. One of the major issues debated was the church policy that bars divorced Catholics who have remarried without seeking a church annulment of their first union from receiving the sacrament of holy communion, a centerpiece of Mass.

(How strictly this ban is observed varies widely, depending on local priests and bishops; plenty of remarried Catholics receive holy communion regularly.)

Getting an annulment requires appearances before a church tribunal and a fee, and it can take years. Francis streamlined the annulment process last year, but for many, it is still an insurmountable obstacle to full participation in the church. Some dioceses, especially in developing countries, do not have such tribunals, which require judges trained in the church's canon law.

At the synods, many bishops insisted that giving communion to divorced Catholics would undermine a core church doctrine that marriage is indissoluble. But other bishops were intent on finding a way to welcome back the divorced.

The second synod ended by essentially allowing both sides to declare victory. However, the dispute reverberated among Catholic intellectuals in the United States, with conservatives warning of an intrachurch civil war.

Now, everyone is looking to Francis to settle the matter. But he may sidestep it, some experts said, by reaffirming church teaching that marriage is permanent, while encouraging flexibility in pastoral practice toward the remarried.

A guide that the Vatican sent to Catholic bishops before the release of "Amoris Laetitia" offered only hints like this: "The pope's concern is therefore to re-contextualize doctrine at the service of the pastoral mission of the church."

M. Cathleen Kaveny, a professor at Boston College who focuses on the relationship between law, religion and morality, said she was expecting "some sort of movement."

"If there is no shift at all, it would have been better had the whole discussion not been opened," she said. "I think that people are looking to Francis to provide some way forward in these intractable personal situations."

THE LAST WORD?

This type of document is a post-synodal apostolic exhortation. The first one to be issued in response to a synod of bishops was in 1967, by Pope Paul VI.

Apostolic exhortations are not as authoritative as papal encyclicals, and they do not normally change church doctrine. But there is doctrine, and there is practice, and the pope's instruction can influence how priests and bishops apply doctrine.

This is Francis' second apostolic exhortation. The first, "Evangelii Gaudium," or "The Joy of the Gospel," was released in 2013, Francis' first year as pope, and it is considered his manifesto. In it, he proclaims that the church must be open and humble to people's real needs, and not too rigidly fixed on doctrine. Many expect to see those themes echoed in the new document.

THE FRANCIS EFFECT?

Francis is one of the world's most popular and influential figures, with a public persona that blends humility with boldness. From the first moments of his papacy, Francis challenged the Vatican hierarchy and took strong stances on issues such as capitalism, poverty, migration and climate change.

But Francis is also deeply pragmatic, particularly regarding internal church politics. Francis may want to be a bold reformer, but he knows the church can be pushed only so far, so quickly, especially given differing opinions among church leaders. He needs the world's bishops to be unified behind him if he wants changes to filter to the parish level.

Yet taking a middle-of-the-road approach is not without risks. Many Catholics eager for the church to change — and in a tangible way — look to him as their change agent. Doing too little may leave some supporters alienated, just as doing too much may anger conservative opponents. It is quite a balancing act.

LAURIE GOODSTEIN, The Times's national religion correspondent for nearly two decades, reported from New York; and **JIM YARDLEY**, who has been covering Pope Francis since his election, reported from Rome, where he is The Times's bureau chief.

Francis' Message Calls on Church to Be Inclusive

BY JIM YARDLEY AND LAURIE GOODSTEIN | APRIL 8, 2016

ROME — In a broad proclamation on family life, Pope Francis on Friday called for the Roman Catholic Church to be more welcoming and less judgmental, and he seemingly signaled a pastoral path for divorced and remarried Catholics to receive holy communion.

The 256-page document — known as an apostolic exhortation and titled "Amoris Laetitia," Latin for "The Joy of Love" — calls for priests to welcome single parents, gay people and unmarried straight couples who are living together.

"A pastor cannot feel that it is enough to simply apply moral laws to those living in 'irregular' situations, as if they were stones to throw at people's lives," he wrote.

But Francis once again closed the door on same-sex marriage, saying it cannot be seen as the equivalent of heterosexual unions.

The document offers no new rules or marching orders, and from the outset Francis makes plain that no top-down edicts are coming.

Alluding to the diversity and complexity of a global church, Francis effectively pushes decision making downward to bishops and priests, stating that a different country or region "can seek solutions better suited to its culture and sensitive to its traditions and local needs."

But Francis also makes clear the vision he wants local bishops and priests to follow: as a church that greets families with empathy and comfort rather than with unbending rules and rigid codes of conduct.

The scope of "Amoris Laetitia" is typical Francis: a broad-ranging blend of biblical passages, meditations on marital love, homespun advice on familial manners, passages bemoaning the frenetic loneliness of modern life and a call for families to come closer to the church, and vice versa.

He admits that the church has made mistakes in alienating families and dedicates many passages to describing the pressures brought on families by poverty, migration, drug abuse and violence.

Just as he used his environmental encyclical, "Laudato Si'," to call on national governments to enact legislation to fight climate change, Francis now calls for governments to provide support for families in the form of health care, education and employment. He describes families as under siege by the pressures of modern life.

"In many cases, parents come home exhausted, not wanting to talk, and many families no longer even share a common meal," Francis wrote. He described "severe stress" on families "who often seem more caught up with securing their future than with enjoying the present."

"This is a broader cultural problem, aggravated by fears about steady employment, finances and the future of children," he wrote.

Although Francis has earned a reputation as a reformer, some liberal Catholics may be disappointed. Many had hoped Francis might go further, perhaps by detailing health exceptions to the ban on contraception, expanding the roles for women in the church or prescribing a clear process that would permit Catholics who divorced and remarried outside the church to receive communion.

"It wasn't as innovative as many had hoped," said Lucetta Scaraffia, a scholar of Catholicism in Rome, adding, "The result is quite modest with respect to the investment and expectations that the world had."

The document is likely to stir debate and disagreement among many Catholics, especially in interpreting the pope's language explaining how priests should work with divorced and remarried Catholics to help them return to full standing in the church.

Francis convened two successive assemblies, or synods, of bishops from around the world to examine the challenges facing modern families.

Synods under Francis' predecessors were relatively sleepy affairs, but Francis told the bishops he wanted them to speak their minds without holding back. And they did.

Both synods were contentious and, the participants said afterward, ultimately enlightening. The battle lines were basically drawn over what it means for the church to be pastoral and merciful in its approach to people who are not living in accord with the Christian ideal of the intact, nuclear family. How far should the church bend to respond to modern life or to bring people back?

Both synods concluded with final reports written by participating bishops, and Francis has drawn extensively on those reports in his exhortation.

Francis adopts the solution introduced by the German-speaking bishops at the second synod: inviting divorced and remarried Catholics who have not had their first marriages annulled to seek the counsel of a priest. The priest, in private and personal conversations known as the "internal forum," could help them to examine their conscience and determine their future participation in church life.

" 'Amoris Laetitia' is a quietly revolutionary document," said the Rev. James Martin, a Jesuit who is editor at large for America magazine. "It restores the role of personal conscience and reminds pastors to meet people where they are. It will be a great encouragement especially to divorced and remarried Catholics and anyone who feels they have been unwelcome in the church. The message is: Welcome."

Conservative Catholics, who have already expressed concern that Francis could destabilize the church and undermine doctrine, were far less impressed. R. R. Reno, a Catholic theologian and editor of First Things, a conservative journal of religion and public life, lamented what he called a "muddy" document that substitutes the church's "rules and laws and requirements" with "talk about ideals and values."

"I think it's an ill-judged shift," Mr. Reno said. "This document clearly opens up the possibility that a priest may determine that a divorced and remarried person is worthy to receive communion, but under what terms and why is muddy."

At a Vatican news conference to unveil the document, Cardinal Christoph Schönborn of Austria said that Francis was trying to erase the distinction between "regular" and "irregular" families, even as he continued to advocate the Christian ideal of marriage.

Cardinal Schönborn, himself the child of divorced parents, said the pope's message is that God's mercy applies to all.

"No one must feel condemned," he said. "No one is scorned."

Cardinal Schönborn noted that Francis' "pervasive principle of inclusion clearly troubles some people," for example those who are concerned that the pope favors a mentality of "anything goes," an allusion to conservative Catholic critics. He argued, however, that the pope is not changing church doctrine on the family but is deepening the understanding outlined by Pope John Paul II in his own document on the family, "Familiaris Consortio."

"It is a classic example of the organic development of doctrine," Cardinal Schönborn said. "There is innovation and continuity."

Homosexuality was another hot-button issue, and Francis took his cues from the majority view in the synods. (During the first synod, an interim report written by a committee of bishops used language that was strikingly welcoming to gay people, but it received so much criticism from other bishops at the synod that it was gone by the final report.)

Echoing the report issued by the second synod in 2015, Francis' exhortation says that "every person regardless of sexual orientation" should be treated with respect and consideration, while "every sign of unjust discrimination is to be carefully avoided, particularly any form of aggression and violence."

But in the next section, he states categorically that the church cannot countenance same-sex marriages or unions, citing the second synod's final report, which said "there are absolutely no grounds for considering homosexual unions to be in any way similar remotely analogous to God's plan for marriage and family."

The document "does not inspire joy in L.G.B.T. Catholics and their supporters," said Francis DeBernardo, the executive director of New Ways Ministry, an advocacy group for gay Catholics.

"While not expecting a blessing on marriage for lesbian and gay couples, many were anticipating that Pope Francis would offer an affirming message to L.G.B.T. people, and not the same ill-informed comments," said Mr. DeBernardo, who is based in Maryland. "Where is the Pope Francis who embraced his gay former student and husband during his U.S. visit? Where is the Pope Francis who invited a transgender Spanish man for a personal meeting at the Vatican? This Pope Francis is hard to find in his latest text."

But this was the rare harsh passage in what is otherwise a fatherly letter to the church. Francis is releasing it during a year he has declared to be a Jubilee of Mercy. At every opportunity, he has been reminding Catholics that forgiveness and mercy are the heart of their faith.

"No one can be condemned forever, because that is not the logic of the Gospel!" the exhortation says. He adds that he is speaking not only of the divorced and remarried, "but of everyone, in whatever situation they find themselves."

ELISABETTA POVOLEDO and **GAIA PIANIGIANI** contributed reporting from Rome.

Pope Francis Shifts Power From Rome With 'Hugely Important' Liturgical Reform

BY JASON HOROWITZ | SEPT. 9, 2017

VATICAN CITY — Pope Francis, who has used his absolute authority in the Vatican to decentralize power from Rome, made a widespread change Saturday to the ways, and words, in which Roman Catholics worship by amending Vatican law to give national bishop conferences greater authority in translating liturgical language.

"It's hugely important," said Rita Ferrone, a specialist in Catholic liturgy who writes for Commonweal, a liberal Catholic magazine. She said that by loosening Rome's grip on the language of prayers, Francis had restored the intention of the reforms of the Second Vatican Council and erased some of the rollbacks of his predecessor, Benedict XVI. "It was especially astute that he put it into canon law because it makes it official."

Francis has not been shy in efforts to reform the church and has tread on some of its most delicate subjects, from challenging the Roman bureaucracy that runs the church to emphasizing acceptance of gays and the divorced.

On Saturday he stepped squarely onto the battlefield of the so-called Liturgy Wars, which, especially in the English-speaking church, have divided liberals and conservatives for decades.

With "Magnum Principium," a papal Motu Proprio — or a document issued under the pope's own legal authority — Francis altered a key 2001 instruction by Pope John Paul II that empowered Vatican officials in Rome to ensure local translations adhered to the standard Latin.

Catholic progressives have advocated a greater use of contemporary idioms consistent with the Second Vatican Council reforms of the

1960s and many bristled under what they considered a heavy and out-of-touch hand from Rome.

Conservative opponents favored the Latin Mass, or at least more faithful translations to it in the local language, and they wanted the church hierarchy in Rome to ensure global universality and unity by making all of those translations uniform.

By amending the Code of Canon Law, Francis appears to have sided with the liberals in the debate and shifted the ownership of translations to the local bishops.

The amendment is a significant development in a liturgical schism that has split Catholics across the world and was evident at the highest echelons of the church.

In 2007, Benedict himself issued a Motu Proprio increasing access to the celebration of the traditional Latin Mass, a move seen as a microcosm of the church's shift toward traditionalism during his papacy.

In changing the law, which will go into effect on Oct. 1, the pope recalled that the Vatican Council entrusted bishops with the "weighty task of introducing the vernacular language into the liturgy." He added that "in order that the renewal of the whole liturgical life might continue, it seemed opportune that some principles handed on since the time of the council should be more clearly reaffirmed and put into practice."

He also acknowledged the bitter feelings that the fights over liturgical language have produced, writing, "It is no surprise that difficulties have arisen" between local churches and the Vatican. He then called for "reciprocal trust" between the local churches and the Vatican department with liturgical oversight, known as the Congregation for Divine Worship and the Discipline of the Sacraments.

But Vatican observers say trust is in short supply between the pope and the cardinal he selected in 2014 to run the department, Robert Sarah.

A hero to Vatican conservatives — and for many, a desired candidate in the next conclave to choose a new pope — Cardinal Sarah has been undermined by partisans of Francis who have worked on a committee to loosen the Guinean cardinal's cherished Latin literalism.

In 2016, Cardinal Sarah called for priests to celebrate Mass ad orientem, or with their backs to the congregation. Francis promptly issued an unusual public rebuke. And in April of this year, Cardinal Sarah sent a letter honoring Benedict's support of the Latin Mass, asserting that "modern liturgy" had caused devastation and schism. Benedict wrote that "the liturgy is in good hands," in an afterward to a book the cardinal wrote this year.

But the liturgy seems to have been in the hands of Francis all along.

Saturday's Vatican announcement was made as the pope visited Medellin, Colombia, the site of a landmark 1968 meeting that emphasized local Latin American influence in church decision-making. It also came just weeks after the pope — not one to invoke his magisterial authority — did just that when he announced that the liturgical reform of the Second Vatican Council was "irreversible."

VIZZOR IMAGE/LATINCONTENT EDITORIAL/GETTY IMAGES

Pope Francis celebrates a Holy Mass as part of his apostolic five-day visit to Colombia.

Progressive interpretations of those reforms in the 1960s provoked a backlash, and a "reform of the reform" movement, which ultimately had advocates at the top of the church during the reigns of John Paul II and Pope Benedict XVI.

In 2001, the Vatican issued the Liturgiam Authenticam, or Authentic Liturgy, instructing that translations from Latin needed to be "in the most exact manner, without omissions or additions in terms of their content."

That same year, the Vatican established Vox Clara, or Clear Voice, a committee to scrutinize English-language translations of the texts and prayers included in the Roman Missal. The committee advocated a close fidelity to the Latin.

In 2006, the Vatican successfully pressured American bishops to accept a more literal translation of well-known English prayers. In 2011, many English-speaking priests panned their effort, finding the language clunky and archaic.

While noting the unity instilled by the Roman Rite, Francis argued for the beauty and accessibility of local languages. He wrote on Saturday that "vernacular languages themselves, often only in a progressive manner, would be able to become liturgical languages, standing out in a not dissimilar way to liturgical Latin for their elegance of style and the profundity of their concepts with the aim of nourishing the faith."

Lost in Translation? Pope Ponders an Update to Lord's Prayer

BY ELISABETTA POVOLEDO, LAURIE GOODSTEIN AND ALAN COWELL | DEC. 8, 2017

ROME — It has been a question of theological debate and liturgical interpretation for years, and now Pope Francis has joined the discussion: Does the Lord's Prayer, Christendom's resonant petition to the Almighty, need an update?

In a new television interview, Pope Francis said the common rendering of one line in the prayer — "lead us not into temptation" — was "not a good translation" from ancient texts. "Do not let us fall into temptation," he suggested, might be better because God does not lead people into temptation; Satan does.

"A father doesn't do that," the pope said. "He helps you get up right away. What induces into temptation is Satan."

In essence, the pope said, the prayer, from the Book of Matthew, is asking God, "When Satan leads us into temptation, You please, give me a hand."

French Catholics adopted such a linguistic change this week, and the pope suggested that Italian Catholics might want to follow suit.

While Francis' remarks were not a decree to change the prayer, he has once again set off a debate on how far a pope can or should go in shaking up longstanding tradition, and even doctrine.

He has already angered Catholic traditionalists by reconsidering the prohibition on granting communion to the divorced and remarried, and by taking on issues like climate change and economic inequality, as well as with famously freewheeling remarks like "who am I to judge?" about gay people.

Francis' idea on changing the Lord's Prayer could unsettle some Catholics, who learn from childhood to recite the prayer, also called the "Our Father."

Philip F. Lawler, editor of Catholic World News, a conservative website, said that while the pope's critique about the translation of the line "isn't unreasonable," if Francis actually intends to change the prayer, "it's very upsetting" because it is so deeply ingrained for Catholics.

"Pope Francis has made a habit of saying things that throw people into confusion, and this is one of them," Mr. Lawler said. "It just makes you wonder, where does it stop, what's up for grabs. It's cumulative unease."

Some conservative evangelicals were also quick to respond.

"I was shocked and appalled," R. Albert Mohler Jr., president of the Southern Baptist Theological Seminary, said in a phone interview. "This is the Lord's Prayer. It is not, and has never been, the pope's prayer, and we have the very words of Jesus in the New Testament. It is those very words that the pope proposes to change. It is not only deeply problematic, it's almost breathtaking."

A commentary on the website of TV2000, the ecclesiastical television station in Rome that interviewed the pope, acknowledged that the pope's words had stirred controversy. But it said, "it is worth recalling that this question is not new."

"This is not a mere whim for Francis," it added.

The basic question, the commentary said, is whether God brings humans into temptation or whether "it is human weakness to surrender to the blandishments of the evil one."

Francis recently took the controversial step of changing church law to give local bishops' conferences more authority over translations of the liturgy. He was responding, in part, to widespread discontent with English translations that were literally correct but awkward and unfamiliar for worshipers.

On Sunday, French churches began using a version of the Lord's Prayer in which the line "Ne nous soumets pas à la tentation" (roughly, "do not expose us to temptation") was replaced with "Ne nous laisse pas entrer en tentation" ("do not let us give in to temptation").

The new French version had been discussed for several years, according to Guy de Kerimel, bishop of Grenoble, who said the previous wording was "often misunderstood by believers," as many parishioners interpreted it to mean that God himself was responsible for the temptation that leads men to sin.

Other French-speaking churches have already made the switch to newer wording. In Belgium and Benin, the revised Lord's Prayer was introduced earlier this year. The United Protestant Church of France also validated the change during its national synod in 2016.

The Church of England has two forms of the Lord's Prayer — traditional and contemporary — but both use the same wording in seeking protection from temptation, according to the church's website.

The pope's reflection was part of a nine-episode commentary on the Lord's Prayer that TV2000, which is owned by the Italian conference of Roman Catholic bishops, has broadcast every Wednesday evening since October.

Each program includes an exchange between the Pope and the Rev. Marco Pozza, a prison chaplain in Padua known as "Father Spritz," after the renowned Venetian aperitif, because of his work evangelizing young people in bars and on the streets.

In a book published in connection with the program, the pope said: "Evil is not something impalpable that spreads like the fog of Milan. It's a person, Satan."

Satan is a master of seduction, the pope added, and that, in the end, "is the meaning of the verse, 'Do not let us fall into evil.' We must be crafty in the good sense of the word, we must be sharp, have the ability to discern the lies of Satan with whom, I am convinced, it's not possible to conduct a dialogue."

ELISABETTA POVOLEDO reported from Rome, **LAURIE GOODSTEIN** from New York and **ALAN COWELL** from London. Reporting was contributed by **DAPHNÉ ANGLÈS** and **ELOISE STARK** from Paris, **MELISSA EDDY** from Berlin, and **SEWELL CHAN** from New York.

Pope Francis Puts Caring for Migrants and Opposing Abortion on Equal Footing

BY JASON HOROWITZ | APRIL 9, 2018

VATICAN CITY — Caring for migrants and the poor is as holy a pursuit as opposing abortion, Pope Francis declared in a major document issued by the Vatican on Monday morning.

Pushing back against conservative critics within the church who argue that the 81-year-old pope's focus on social issues has led him to lose sight of the true doctrine, Pope Francis again cast himself, and the mission of the Roman Catholic Church, in a more progressive light.

"The other harmful ideological error is found in those who find suspect the social engagement of others, seeing it as superficial, worldly, secular, materialist, communist or populist," Pope Francis wrote in an apostolic exhortation on the subject of holiness issued Monday morning. "Our defense of the innocent unborn, for example, needs to be clear, firm and passionate. Equally sacred, however, are the lives of the poor, those already born, the destitute, the abandoned."

The pope's vision of holiness explicitly highlights migrants, whose plight he has sought to elevate to global attention perhaps more than any other issue.

"We often hear it said that, with respect to relativism and the flaws of our present world, the situation of migrants, for example, is a lesser issue," he said. "Some Catholics consider it a secondary issue compared to the 'grave' bioethical questions."

"That a politician looking for votes might say such a thing is understandable, but not a Christian," he continued, adding that welcoming the stranger at the door was fundamental to the faith. "This is not a notion invented by some Pope, or a momentary fad."

NURPHOTO/GETTY IMAGES

Pope Francis celebrates Mass in St. Peter's Square on the Sunday of Divine Mercy.

The pope's 103-page document — an apostolic exhortation titled "Gaudete et Exsultate," or "Rejoice and Be Glad" — is less authoritative than a papal encyclical, but is nevertheless an important teaching pronouncement. At its outset, Francis makes clear that it is not meant "to be a treatise on holiness" but to "re-propose the call to holiness in a practical way for our own time."

As he put it elsewhere in the document, "Seeing and acting with mercy: That is holiness." That statement is a distilled expression of Francis' vision of the church, which is consistent with a view articulated by Cardinal Joseph L. Bernardin, the archbishop of Chicago who died in 1996, and who called for a "consistent ethic of life" that wove issues of life and social justice into a "seamless garment."

The pope is reminding his church to "expand our view," said Archbishop Angelo De Donatis, the vicar general of Rome.

Throughout the document, Francis urges followers to be less consumed with showy demonstrations of faith and piousness than with patiently and lovingly raising children, working hard to support families and representing what he called "the middle class of holiness."

"In their daily perseverance, I see the holiness of the Church militant," Francis wrote, using a phrase that has been appropriated by archconservatives critical of his papacy. The pope's allies have described the fringe Catholic website Church Militant as openly in favor of political "ultraconservatism."

But a majority of the document is a rumination on what constitutes an effective and true practice of holiness.

While he says "the silence of prolonged prayer" is critical, Francis adds that holiness at times requires the faithful to be loud and active, and says it "is not healthy" to seek prayer while disdaining service.

He cautions against a cold reason untethered from spirituality, and warns against an overemphasis on the power of human will alone, "as if it were something pure, perfect, all-powerful, to which grace is then added."

In doing so, he suggests that prosperity and power gospels fail to realize that not everyone can do everything. Holiness requires humility, he says, and a lack of "acknowledgment of our limitations prevents grace from working more effectively within us."

In a section of the document titled "Signs of Holiness in Today's World," the pope explicitly laments a modern culture that includes "the self-content bred by consumerism; individualism; and all those forms of ersatz spirituality — having nothing to do with God — that dominate the current religious marketplace."

The pope, like many others, is also worried that social networks like Facebook feed into the hedonism and consumerism that "can prove our downfall" and are, in short, a waste of time.

"When we allow ourselves to be caught up in superficial information, instant communication and virtual reality, we can waste precious time," he says, adding that "all of us, but especially the young, are immersed in a culture of zapping."

At a news conference introducing the exhortation Monday afternoon, the Vatican presented a promotional video in which a mediocre and unholy life was illustrated by a young man playing video games, while a holy life was living joyfully with one's family. But the video, like Francis, most emphasized the need to care for the poor and to welcome migrants.

To highlight that point, the Vatican offered interviews with Mohammad Jawad Haidari, a Muslim refugee from Afghanistan. Asked what he thought about the pope explicitly putting the care for migrants on the same footing as opposition to abortion, he said, "It was a surprise, and a revolutionary text with respect of the vision I had before of the Christian world."

Conservatives inside the Vatican have argued for years that the pope is leading the faithful astray, especially with a previous apostolic exhortation — "Amoris Laetitia," or "The Joy of Love" — that signaled a pastoral path for divorced and remarried Catholics to receive holy communion.

That possibility, which critics have called heretical and schismatic, has been a rallying cry for a small but committed group of traditionalists.

When asked if the document on holiness was a response to those critics, the panelists at the Vatican news conference on Monday, including Archbishop De Donatis, looked uncomfortably at one other for several seconds before giving a roundabout answer.

But some of the passages seemed intended as a rebuke to the canon lawyers and archconservative cardinals leading the opposition to Pope Francis.

In the document, the pope excoriates Christians taking the path of "an obsession with the law, an absorption with social and political advantages, a punctilious concern for the Church's liturgy, doctrine and prestige." They should instead be passionate about "seeking out the lost," he writes.

He is also withering in his criticism of the hostile tenor that often reverberates throughout the conservative Catholic blogosphere.

"Christians, too, can be caught up in networks of verbal violence through the internet," Francis said, citing vicious examples of defamation in some Catholic outlets where "people look to compensate for their own discontent by lashing out at others." He adds that in upholding some commandments, they ignore the forbidding of bearing false witness and vilification. "Here we see how the unguarded tongue, set on fire by hell, sets all things ablaze," he says.

The pope has been less critical of his liberal interlocutors, including those who sometimes put words in his mouth. One favorite, if infamously unreliable, narrator of the pope's conversations, recently caused a controversy when he asserted that the pontiff did not believe in hell.

But in "Rejoice and Be Glad," Francis indicated that he had no doubt the devil is real.

"We should not think of the devil as a myth, a representation, a symbol, a figure of speech or an idea," he writes. "This mistake would lead us to let down our guard."

In the devil's arsenal is the spreading of gossip, which the pope disdains, but he also expresses an intolerance for the intolerant and close-minded.

In another poke at conservative critics inside the Vatican hierarchy, he bemoans those who would prefer a self-righteous and orthodox minority to the tough work of spreading peace by embracing "even those who are a bit odd, troublesome or difficult."

"Sowing peace all around us," he writes. "That is holiness."

CHAPTER 3

The Church, Social Issues and a Changing World

The Catholic church has been historically reluctant to change its core positions on social issues such as acceptance of L.G.B.T.Q. individuals, abortion and divorce. Church leaders invested in economic justice have also not had progressive inclinations regarding birth control or euthanasia. While not changing official church doctrine, Pope Francis' public remarks on social issues have signaled greater acceptance of L.G.B.T.Q. individuals than his predecessors. This shift has contributed to Francis' conflict with American Catholics in particular.

On Gay Priests, Pope Francis Asks, 'Who Am I to Judge?'

BY RACHEL DONADIO | JULY 29, 2013

ROME — For generations, homosexuality has largely been a taboo topic for the Vatican, ignored altogether or treated as "an intrinsic moral evil," in the words of the previous pope.

In that context, brief remarks by Pope Francis suggesting that he would not judge priests for their sexual orientation, made aboard the papal airplane on the way back from his first foreign trip, to Brazil, resonated through the church. Never veering from church doctrine opposing homosexuality, Francis did strike a more compassionate tone than that of his predecessors, some of whom had largely avoided even saying the more colloquial "gay."

"If someone is gay and he searches for the Lord and has good will, who am I to judge?" Francis told reporters, speaking in Italian but using the English word "gay."

Francis' words could not have been more different from those of Benedict XVI, who in 2005 wrote that homosexuality was "a strong tendency ordered toward an intrinsic moral evil," and an "objective disorder." The church document said men with "deep-seated homosexual tendencies" should not become priests.

Vatican experts were quick to point out that Francis was not suggesting that the priests or anyone else should act on their homosexual tendencies, which the church considers a sin. But the fact that he made such comments — and used the word "gay" — was nevertheless revolutionary, and likely to generate significant discussion in local dioceses, where bishops are divided over whether to accept priests who are gay but celibate.

"It's not a great opening in terms of contents, but the fact that he talked about it that way is a great novelty," said Paolo Rodari, a Vatican expert at the Italian daily La Repubblica. Francis would probably agree with Benedict's writings on homosexuality, he added, "but it doesn't interest him."

"It interests him to say that the problem in the end isn't if someone has this tendency, the important thing is to live in the light of God," Mr. Rodari said. "Said by a pope, it's enormous."

Francis also told reporters that while Pope John Paul II had definitively closed the door to female priests, he sought a "theology of women" and a greater role for them in Catholic life, news reports said.

The pope's comments on homosexuals and women in the church were yet another sign of the different directions from which Benedict and Francis approach doctrine. While Benedict, the shy theologian, focused more on ethics and advocated a purer church, even if it might end up being smaller, Francis was elected for his belief that the

Catholic Church must engage in dialogue with the world — even with those it disagrees with — if it wants to stay vibrant and relevant.

"At a certain point, tone becomes substance if it's seen as revitalizing the prospects of the church," said John L. Allen, Jr., a Vatican expert at The National Catholic Reporter.

In Benedict's more subdued 2007 visit to Brazil, where Evangelical churches are making rapid inroads in the Catholic majority, he delivered speeches to bishops about how to respond to postmodern society.

In contrast, Francis spoke on the beach, engaged with the masses and was greeted like a rock star by followers entranced by his approachable style and homespun folksy adages. ("You can always add more water to the beans," he said at one point.)

More than a million people gathered for an open-air Mass on Copacabana Beach on Sunday. At one event, bishops danced on stage to upbeat music. The spectacle was clearly aimed at competing with Evangelical churches that have a more "pop" style.

"We can see the figure of Peter so near to us," said Milena Rocha, 20, a Brazilian student who slept on the beach Saturday night along with thousands of others in a vigil before the pope's final Mass on Sunday, comparing Francis to St. Peter.

She said that the vigil, in which many camped on the sands on pieces of cardboard, showed the energy that Francis was bringing to the church in Brazil, which has more Catholics than any other country, an estimated 123 million.

Despite missteps by organizers, including one that compromised security, the visit unfolded peacefully, giving many people a chance to glimpse or even embrace Francis.

"This pope keeps renewing the church," said Claudia Brandão, 30, a housewife who traveled from Angola with her 9-month-old daughter.

In 2007, "Benedict came and played the standard classical nocturne that he was famous for, and his devotees loved it. Francis came and played the guitar in his very accessible style and the crowds went wild," said Mr. Allen, who traveled to Brazil for both trips.

Before he resigned in February, Benedict's papacy had been marked by scandals — a sexual abuse scandal, a leaks scandal and trouble with the secretive Vatican Bank. Francis, with his style of radical simplicity and his direct manner, has shifted things. "He's completely changed the narrative about the church," Mr. Allen said. "In five months, now the dominant Catholic story is 'Charismatic Pope Takes World by Storm.' "

During his papal trips, John Paul II loved to walk to the back of the plane and chat with reporters, while Benedict only responded to a handful of preselected questions. Francis, on the overnight flight back to Rome from Rio de Janeiro, spoke freely to reporters for 80 minutes about everything from the Vatican Bank troubles to his decision not to live in the Apostolic Palace but rather in a Vatican residence.

Francis did not dodge a single question, even thanking the person who prompted his comments on homosexuality, asking about Italian news reports of a "gay lobby" inside the Vatican, with clerics blackmailing one another with information about sexual missteps.

"So much is written about the gay lobby. I have yet to find on a Vatican identity card the word 'gay,' " Francis said, chuckling. "They say there are some gay people here. I think that when we encounter a gay person, we must make the distinction between the fact of a person being gay and the fact of a lobby, because lobbies are not good."

An article in the Italian weekly L'Espresso this month alleged that one of the advisers that Francis had appointed to look into the Vatican Bank, Msgr. Battista Ricca, had been accused of having gay trysts when he was a Vatican diplomat in Uruguay. The pope told reporters that nothing in the documentation he had seen substantiated the reports.

He added that such a lobby would be an issue, but that he did not have anything against gay people and that their sins should be forgiven like those of all Catholics. Francis said that homosexuals should be treated with dignity, and that no one should be subjected to blackmail or pressure because of sexual orientation.

“The problem isn’t having this orientation. The problem is making a lobby,” he said.

In recent years, both Benedict and Francis have tried to make changes at the Vatican Bank so that it meets international anti-money-laundering norms that are a condition for using the euro.

Asked about the bank, Francis said, “Some say that it’s better to have a bank, others that it would be better to have a fund, still others say to close it.”

Asked what was in the black briefcase that he was seen carrying onto the plane by himself en route to Brazil, Francis said he had a razor, a breviary and a book about St. Teresa. “It’s normal to carry a bag,” he said, according to news reports. “I’m a bit surprised that the image of the bag made its way around the world. Anyway, it wasn’t the suitcase with the codes for the nuclear bomb.”

Pope Francis in Context

OPINION | BY ROSS DOUTHAT | JULY 30, 2013

THE CYCLE IS FAMILIAR: A pope says something about a controversial issue that doesn't fit the media's semi-informed preconceptions about Roman Catholic teaching, a firestorm of coverage follows, and then better-informed observers are left to pick up the pieces and explain that no, actually, the pope is just reasserting an idea — an openness to Darwinian evolution, the possibility that nonbelievers might go to heaven, pick your controversy — that the church already accepted or believed or allowed to be considered.

In the case of Pope Francis' comments on homosexuality on the plane back from a wildly successful World Youth Day in Brazil, though, I have a little more sympathy than usual for the media reaction. Here's what the pontiff said, per the Catholic News Service, in response to a question about sex scandals and a so-called "gay lobby" within the Vatican and the Roman Curia:

> *... Pope Francis said it was important to "distinguish between a person who is gay and someone who makes a gay lobby," he said. "A gay lobby isn't good."*
>
> *"A gay person who is seeking God, who is of good will — well, who am I to judge him?" the pope said. "The Catechism of the Catholic Church explains this very well. It says one must not marginalize these persons, they must be integrated into society. The problem isn't this (homosexual) orientation — we must be like brothers and sisters. The problem is something else, the problem is lobbying either for this orientation or a political lobby or a Masonic lobby."*

Now it's certainly true, as a host of Catholic writers quickly pointed out, that this doesn't depart from official church teaching on human sexuality, and indeed invokes the language of the Catechism (commissioned by John Paul II and overseen by Joseph Ratzinger, the future Benedict XVI) to make its point. Which, means, in turn, that a lot of the more breathless coverage has exaggerated the significance of the pope's words, and overhyped the gap between what he's saying and what his predecessors might have said.

But at the same time, the context of the remarks — the specific subject being addressed, and the larger pattern of Francis' words and deeds — do magnify their significance beyond the "newsflash: pope still Catholic" norm that defines a lot of these soundbite controversies. First, the pope does seem to have been talking specifically about gay Catholics in the priesthood. Indeed, according to this translation, the words quoted above followed a question about the case of Monsignor Battista Ricca, a recent papal appointee with an alleged gay relationship in his past, which inspired Francis to a long riff about the importance of forgiving past sins. And given that Benedict XVI's Vatican specifically reasserted the rule that men with a "deep-seated" attraction to the same sex should not enter holy orders, the tone of Francis' remarks alone — the forgive-and-forget response to a particular case, and the broader "who am I to judge" — does seem striking and newsworthy. Consider, by way of contrast, what Benedict said to Peter Seewald, his longtime interviewer, when asked about the subject of gay priests:

> *It is no secret that there are homosexuals even among priests and monks. Just recently there was a major scandal on account of the homosexual passions of priests in Rome.*
>
> *Homosexuality is incompatible with the priestly vocation. Otherwise, celibacy itself would lose its meaning as a renunciation. It would be extremely dangerous if celibacy became a sort of pretext for bringing people into the priesthood who don't want to get married anyway …*
>
> *But there is no doubt that homosexuality exists in monasteries and among the clergy, if not acted out, then at least in a non-practiced form.*
>
> *Well, that is just one of the miseries of the Church. And the persons who are affected must at least try not to express this inclination actively, in order to remain true to the intrinsic mission of their office.*

The settings are different and the questions are different, and I wouldn't be surprised if the Vatican issued a clarification shortly explaining that the official rules for seminary formation are still very much in effect. But still, such a tonal difference, from "the miseries of the Church" to "who am I to judge," on a fraught, high-profile topic is surely newsworthy, even if the news media inevitably offered misinterpretations of its significance as well.

And it's especially newsworthy since a latitudinarian statement on this topic is of a piece with the tone of Francis' pontificate as a whole. Popes do not change doctrine, but they do choose what to emphasize and what to downplay, which issues to elevate and which to set aside, where to pass judgment and where to talk about forgiveness, and so forth. And we've seen enough of this pontificate to sense where Francis' focus lies: He wants to be seen primarily as a pope of social justice and spiritual renewal, and he doesn't have much patience for issues that might get in the way of that approach to Christian witness. Thus the headline-grabbing rhetoric and symbolic gestures emphasizing poverty and simplicity above all else, thus the frequent invocations of "clericalism" as the worst problem facing the church, thus his fairly casual attitude (in his off-the-cuff remarks, at least) toward doctrinal discipline, his frequent calls for experimentation and his apparent hostility to liturgical traditionalism — and thus, too, his apparent determination to distance himself and his message from the culture-war issues of the post-sexual revolution West.

Again, it's not that Benedict or John Paul actually prioritized issues like abortion and gay marriage over the church's social teaching (Benedict, too, visited prisoners and wrote encyclicals critiquing global capitalism and so on ...), and it's not that Francis is somehow doing the impossible and repudiating church teaching on those hot-button topics. It's just that he's going out of his way to place his emphasis on other issues and areas and concerns, and taking clear steps to avoid the kind of "pope versus sex" headlines that so often dominate coverage of the church. (It's noteworthy, for instance, that in the same post-Brazil interview, he was asked why he didn't address that country's abortion and marriage controversies during his visit, and he answered that "the church already has spoken on these issues," and "young people understand perfectly what the church's point of view is.")

It seems a bit early and a bit presumptuous to offer any kind of judgment on what all this might mean for the church as a whole. To admirers of the previous pope's labors, necessary and often thankless, to preserve the core of Catholic faith, it can be a little painful to watch journalists overhype the contrast between Francis and Benedict (much as they overhyped — and often misjudged — the contrast between Benedict and John Paul), and use Francis' different style to write a "progressive pope, reactionary pope" morality play that doesn't really fit the facts. At the same time, the issues Francis wants to emphasize lie at the very heart of Christianity, and it is no bad thing for conservative Catholics — especially American conservative Catholics — to think and walk with a pope so focused on the poor. Nor is it a bad thing, in the wake of the sex abuse scandals, to have a pope who persuades reporters to tell a story about Catholicism that doesn't begin and end with the sins of priests and the cover-ups of bishops.

I recommend reading Elizabeth Scalia and Damian Thompson, both Benedict fans, for more on these and related issues. Let me conclude, though, by striking a cautionary note about Pope Francis' rhetoric and what it might mean for the governance of the church. I mentioned above the remarks about forgiveness that followed a question about a scandal involving one of his appointees; here they are in full:

> *I'd like to add that many times we seem to seek out the sins of somebody's youth and publish them. We're not talking about crimes, which are something else. The abuse of minors, for instance, is a crime. But one can sin and then convert, and the Lord both forgives and forgets. We don't have the right to refuse to forget ... it's dangerous. The theology of sin is important. St. Peter committed one of the greatest sins, denying Christ, and yet they made him pope. Think about that."*

This is a striking and deeply Christian passage, and the fact that it inspired a Wonkblog meditation (!) on the theology of forgiveness is a testament to Francis' ability to reach unexpected audiences with his rhetoric. But for anyone who followed the deep history of the sex abuse scandal, it has some troubling implications — because much of what went wrong in the church, in the 1960s and 1970s especially, represented a disastrous misapplication of precisely this message. Christianity and Catholicism insist that no sin is beyond forgiveness, and that true repentance washes away even the worst stain. But for people in positions of ecclesiastical authority, the obligation to forgive and forget is complicated by the obligation to protect the faithful and satisfy the demands of justice ... and too often, far too often, the theology of forgiveness was invoked by authority figures in Catholicism as a justification for returning priests to ministry, for hoping that pathologies could be cured in the confessional, and then for refusing to do the appropriate thing when confronted with the consequences of these decisions and resign. The sex abuse disaster was a disaster in part for very worldly reasons, involving clerical privilege and the institutional tendency to cover-up. But it was also a disaster because of misapplied Christian theology, which persuaded many churchmen that the confessional was a sufficient response to both others' evil and their own misgovernment. It was indeed a scandal of clericalism, as the current pope has suggested — but it was clericalism compounded by cheap grace.

Now Francis did specifically exempt crimes against children from his call for a forgiveness that also forgets. But the danger facing the church in the future is not an exact replay of the sex abuse scandal. Rather, it's a perpetuation of a model of church governance in which any scandal — sexual, financial, you name it — is met with forgiveness but not with penance, with apologies but not accountability.

And I raise this point only because for all that Francis has done, as Thompson puts it, to "decontaminate the Catholic brand," where reform is concerned his (yes, brief) papacy has thus far been longer on rhetoric and symbolism than action. There has been no noticeable housecleaning in the hierarchy, and the badly-needed reform of the Curia — the agenda that Francis was elected to implement — is in the hands of a commission, which in Rome as in Washington can bury an issue as often as it actually resolves it. As much as the church needs a pope capable of transcending the church's recent disasters, it also still needs real accountability and real reform — and it does not need another charismatic leader, a la John Paul II, who rallies throngs around the world but neglects the administration of the Vatican. Nor does it need a pope whose media-friendly persona persuades journalists to lay off the church on the one front where a hostile press has often been correct to hold Catholicism to account.

"I believe this is a time of mercy," Pope Francis said, during the same plane conversation. To which I would say yes, but please God, of discipline as well.

ROSS DOUTHAT is an Op-Ed columnist for The New York Times.

The Pope and the Right

OPINION | BY ROSS DOUTHAT | NOV. 30, 2013

"NOW IT'S YOUR TURN to be part of the loyal opposition," a fellow Catholic journalist said to me earlier this year, as Pope Francis' agenda was beginning to take shape.

The friend was a political liberal and lifelong Democrat, accustomed to being on the wrong side of his church's teaching on issues like abortion, bioethics and same-sex marriage.

Now, he cheerfully suggested, right-leaning Catholics like me would get a taste of the same experience, from a pope who seemed intent on skirting the culture war and stressing the church's mission to the poor instead.

After Francis' latest headline-making exhortation, which roves across the entire life of the church but includes a sharp critique of consumer capitalism and financial laissez-faire, politically conservative Catholics have reached for several explanations for why my friend is wrong, and why they aren't the new "cafeteria Catholics."

First, they have pointed out that there's nothing truly novel here, apart from a lazy media narrative that pits Good Pope Francis against his bad reactionary predecessors. (Many of the new pope's comments track with what Benedict XVI said in his own economic encyclical, and with past papal criticisms of commercial capitalism's discontents.)

Second, they have sought to depoliticize the pope's comments, recasting them as a general brief against avarice and consumerism rather than a call for specific government interventions.

And finally, they have insisted on the difference between church teaching on faith and morals, and papal pronouncements on economic issues, noting that there's nothing that obliges Catholics to believe the pontiff is infallible on questions of public policy.

All three responses have their merits, but they still seem insufficient to the Francis era's challenge to Catholics on the limited-government, free-market right.

It's true that there is far more continuity between Francis and Benedict than media accounts suggest. But the new pope clearly intends to foreground the church's social teaching in new ways, and probably seeks roughly the press coverage he's getting.

It's also true that Francis' framework is pastoral rather than political. But his plain language tilts leftward in ways that no serious reader can deny.

Finally, it's true that there is no Catholic position on, say, the correct marginal tax rate, and that Catholics are not obliged to heed the pope when he suggests that global inequality is increasing when the statistical evidence suggests otherwise.

But the church's social teaching is no less an official teaching for allowing room for disagreement on its policy implications. And for Catholics who pride themselves on fidelity to Rome, the burden is on them — on us — to explain why a worldview that inspires left-leaning papal rhetoric also allows for right-of-center conclusions.

That explanation rests, I think, on three ideas. First, that when it comes to lifting the poor out of poverty, global capitalism, faults and all, has a better track record by far than any other system or approach.

Second, that Catholic social teaching, properly understood, emphasizes both solidarity and subsidiarity — that is, a small-c conservative preference for local efforts over national ones, voluntarism over bureaucracy.

Third, that on recent evidence, the most expansive welfare states can crowd out what Christianity considers the most basic human goods — by lowering birthrates, discouraging private charity and restricting the church's freedom to minister in subtle but increasingly consequential ways.

This Catholic case for limited government, however, is not a case for the Ayn Randian temptation inherent to a capitalism-friendly politics. There is no Catholic warrant for valorizing entrepreneurs at the expense of ordinary workers, or for dismissing all regulation as unnecessary and all redistribution as immoral.

And this is where Francis' vision should matter to American Catholics who usually cast ballots for Republican politicians. The pope's words shouldn't inspire them to convert en masse to liberalism, or to worry that the throne of Peter has been seized by a Marxist anti-pope. But they should encourage a much greater integration of Catholic and conservative ideas than we've seen since "compassionate conservatism" collapsed, and inspire Catholics to ask more — often much more — of the Republican Party, on a range of policy issues.

Here my journalist friend's "loyal opposition" line oversimplified the options for Catholic political engagement. His Catholic liberalism didn't go into eclipse because it failed to let the Vatican dictate every jot and tittle of its social agenda. Rather, it lost influence because it failed to articulate any kind of clear Catholic difference, within the bigger liberal tent, on issues like abortion, sex and marriage.

Now the challenge for conservative Catholics is to do somewhat better in our turn, and to spend the Francis era not in opposition but seeking integration — meaning an economic vision that remains conservative, but in the details reminds the world that our Catholic faith comes first.

ROSS DOUTHAT is an Op-Ed columnist for The New York Times.

A Vatican Shot Across the Bow for Hard-Line U.S. Catholics

BY JASON HOROWITZ | AUG. 2, 2017

VATICAN CITY — Two close associates of Pope Francis have accused American Catholic ultraconservatives of making an alliance of "hate" with evangelical Christians to back President Trump, further alienating a group already out of the Vatican's good graces.

The authors, writing in a Vatican-vetted journal, singled out Stephen K. Bannon, Mr. Trump's chief strategist, as a "supporter of an apocalyptic geopolitics" that has stymied action against climate change and exploited fears of migrants and Muslims with calls for "walls and purifying deportations."

The article warns that conservative American Catholics have strayed dangerously into the deepening political polarization in the United States. The writers even declare that the worldview of American evangelical and hard-line Catholics, which is based on a literal interpretation of the Bible, is "not too far apart" from jihadists.

It is not clear if the article, appearing in La Civiltà Cattolica, received the pope's direct blessing, but it was extraordinary coming from a journal that carries the Holy See's seal of approval. There has apparently been no reprimand from the pope, who is not shy about disciplining dissenters, and La Civiltà Cattolica's editor has promoted the article nearly every day since it was published in July.

The article and the backlash to it — accusations of anti-Americanism have been rife, and one prominent American prelate likened the authors to "useful idiots" — have highlighted the widening distance between Francis and American Catholic conservatives.

Since the 2013 election of Pope Francis, conservatives have worried that he has given short shrift to the social issues that have animated them, among them abortion and same-sex marriage. They have sat through his warnings to steer clear of politics. They have watched warily as Francis has installed pastors in his image while sidelining conservative leaders.

It is no secret that Francis, the first Latin American pope, who has often criticized capitalism, has a complicated view of his old neighbors to the north.

Not long after Francis' election, Vatican ambassadors briefed the pontiff about various situations around the world and suggested that he be especially careful when appointing bishops and cardinals in the United States.

"I know that already," the pope interrupted, according to a high-ranking Vatican official familiar with the details of the conversation, who asked that his name not be used while discussing internal Vatican deliberations. "That's where the opposition is coming from."

The Vatican declined to comment about the conversation.

TODD HEISLER/THE NEW YORK TIMES

Pope Francis in Philadelphia during his visit to the United States in 2015. Francis' personnel decisions on the Catholic hierarchy are key to his effort to remake the church, particularly in America.

Fans of the article said it made clear that the conservatives who ran the American church for decades were out of step with the new Catholic mainstream under Francis.

Massimo Faggioli, a professor of historical theology at Villanova University and a contributor to liberal Catholic journals, said the Civiltà Cattolica article would "be remembered in church history as one of the most important to understand the Vatican of Francis and the United States and American Catholicism."

American Catholicism, he argued, echoing the article's thesis, "has become different than mainstream European Catholicism and mainstream Latin American Catholicism," and has fallen "into the hands of the religious right."

The authors of the article argue that American evangelical and ultraconservative Catholics risk corrupting the Roman Catholic faith with an ideology intended to inject "religious influence in the political sphere." They suggest that so-called values voters are using the banners of religious liberty and opposition to abortion to try to supplant secularism with a "theocratic type of state."

Even before the article was published, many Catholic supporters of Mr. Trump, who won the white Catholic vote, were already wary of Francis for suggesting during the campaign that Mr. Trump was "not Christian" because of his preference for building walls rather than bridges.

Francis' apparent openness on key issues such as granting communion to Catholics remarried outside the church has galvanized the opposition, led by the American cardinal Raymond L. Burke, an outspoken critic whom Francis has repeatedly demoted.

The essay, which critics have dismissed as woefully ignorant of religion's deep history in American politics, has energized camps on both sides of the divide. In a Breitbart article headlined "Papal Advisers Bash American Christians in Bigoted Screed," Thomas Williams, the site's Rome correspondent and an associate of Mr. Bannon's, wrote that instead of attacking Mr. Trump and Mr. Bannon, "they have ended up attacking America itself."

Benjamin Harnwell, a Catholic traditionalist in Rome, fan of Mr. Bannon and confidant of Cardinal Burke's, said the article's authors were doing little more than "trolling Steve Bannon." Mr. Bannon, a former altar boy who once articulated his worldview to a Vatican conference, wrote in a brief email that the pope's associates "lit me up."

Archbishop Charles J. Chaput of Philadelphia, a standard-bearer for conservatism in America, likened the Civiltà Cattolica authors in his weekly newsletter to the "useful idiots" who supported the Bolshevik Revolution in Russia. He called the article "an exercise in dumbing down and inadequately presenting the nature of Catholic/evangelical cooperation on religious freedom and other key issues."

If Archbishop Chaput's own thwarted ambitions are any indication, Francis might not agree. The pope has vexed conservatives by repeatedly declining to elevate Archbishop Chaput to the rank of cardinal, a requirement for entrance into the conclave that will choose the pontiff's successor.

"I was a little bit disappointed," Cardinal Gerhard Müller, a German conservative appointed by Pope Benedict XVI as the church's chief doctrinal watchdog, said in a recent interview. "The appointment of the cardinals should not be a personal relation with the pope's to these bishops," he said, adding that he was puzzled as to why Francis passed them over. "I don't know," he said. "Politics."

In July, Francis fired Cardinal Müller.

Personnel decisions in the Catholic hierarchy are crucial to Francis' effort to make the church more inclusive, particularly in the United States.

American Catholic conservatives once unacquainted with being out of papal favor have stewed privately and expressed horror publicly on numerous right-wing Catholic blogs. They accuse Francis of wrecking the church and diluting its doctrine.

Liberal American Catholics, bruised by crackdowns under John Paul II and Benedict XVI, are less than sympathetic to conservative complaints and have felt emboldened by Francis. They are delighted with the pope's promotion of figures like Cardinal Blase J. Cupich of Chicago, who has started a program against gun violence and opposed Republican health care proposals on the ground that they would strip coverage for the weak and poor. Francis chose him to lead the Chicago diocese in 2014, after the retirement of Cardinal Francis George, a giant of American Catholic conservatism, and elevated him to cardinal last year.

"We should speak in a way that invites people and creates a sense of unity in society," Cardinal Cupich said in an interview at the Vatican on the day of his elevation.

Some progressive Catholics have even begun expressing a previously tacit resentment of the hard-right zeal of evangelical, Calvinist and Protestant converts to Catholicism, among them Newt Gingrich, the husband of Callista Gingrich, the new American ambassador to the Holy See.

"I am so tired of converts telling us that the pope is not Catholic," Michael Sean Winters wrote last week in the newspaper National Catholic Reporter.

That deep suspicion of evangelical fundamentalism and the fear of politicization corroding the conservative hierarchy of the American Catholic church was laid bare by the article in La Civiltà Cattolica. The authors were the Rev. Antonio Spadaro, the journal's editor, who is a confidant of Francis'; and Marcelo Figueroa, an Argentine Presbyterian minister who is a friend and longtime collaborator of the pope's.

In an interview, Father Spadaro — whose critics have called him "the pope's mouthpiece" — said the reaction to the essay had been "incredible." He said he had received kind words but also "plenty of hate."

Some critics, he said, had tried to distort the argument into an attack on cooperation between Catholics and Protestants, something he said he himself had promoted. That criticism, he said, often came from opponents of Francis "who are trying to downplay the role of this pontificate."

Father Spadaro would not say whether he had received Francis' approval, or whether he had spoken with the pope since the essay's publication.

The main point of the article, he said, was the pope's argument that religion in the service of politics or power is ideology, and that the manipulation of anxiety for political ends risks rendering the church a "sect of the pure."

Father Spadaro cited, by way of example, the fringe Catholic website Church Militant, which the essay described as openly in favor of political "ultraconservatism." (A related site responded under the headline "Evil Editor of La Civiltà Cattolica Attacks Church Militant.")

Father Spadaro also said it was important to explore the "apocalyptic narrative which inspires" Mr. Bannon, who has digested the works of often anti-Christian right-wing writers such as Julius Evola, who contend that people had drifted away from a primordial, heroic truth.

Father Spadaro said he was alarmed by the retrofitting of a mystical apocalyptical worldview into conservative Catholicism.

"We are warning against this kind of mixture, which is dangerous," he said.

The Vatican's America Problem

OPINION | BY ROSS DOUTHAT | AUG. 2, 2017

IN 1892, POPE LEO XIII addressed a letter to the Catholics of France. For a century French politics had been divided between mostly Catholic monarchists and mostly anticlericalist republicans, and the church had championed royalists against the secular republic. But now the pope urged French Catholics to take a different approach — to rally to the republic, a strategy called "ralliement," and work through republican institutions to protect the church's liberties and promote the common good.

In European politics this was a novel gambit, but for American Catholics at the time it amounted to a tacit endorsement of what they were already doing. In the United States there was no ancien regime to imagine restoring, no plausible scenario in which the integration of

STEPHEN CROWLEY/THE NEW YORK TIMES

Supporters of Donald Trump at a campaign rally in Cincinnati, Ohio, Oct. 13, 2016.

church and state might be achieved — and Catholics had been trying to prove their patriotism in a largely Protestant country by rallying to the republic since the founding era.

So Leo's letter began a long (and complicated) process of harmonization between America and Rome, sealed in the 1960s at the Second Vatican Council, in which the church's political thought was tacitly Americanized. No more would the Vatican emphasize the necessity, for Catholics, of supporting an "integralist" relationship between their government and church. Instead the American way of doing religious politics — in which a secular political framework allowed a great deal of room for religiously inspired activism — was blessed and accepted as the Catholic way as well.

Over the last decade, however, as American Christianity has weakened and American politics become ever-more-polarized, the Catholic position in the United States has become more difficult and perplexing. The Democratic Party, whose long-ago New Deal was built in part on Catholic social thought, has become increasingly secular and ever-more-doctrinaire in its social liberalism. The Republican Party, which under George W. Bush wrapped the Catholic-inflected language of "compassionate conservatism" around its pro-life commitments, has been pinballing between an Ayn Rand-ish libertarianism and the white identity politics of the Trump era.

As a result a sense of disillusionment and homelessness among Catholic thinkers — younger ones, especially — has increased. It isn't just that old 20th century approaches to Catholic politics — both the ethnic-Catholic liberalism of a Mario Cuomo or a Ted Kennedy and the Catholic neoconservatism that shaped figures like Jeb Bush and Marco Rubio or Paul Ryan — seem like they're out of energy and influence. It's also that Western liberalism writ large seems at once hostile to traditional religion and beset by internal contradictions, making the moment ripe for serious Catholic rethinking, a new and perhaps even post-liberal Catholic politics.

So far that new thinking includes revivals of radicalism on the

Catholic left, where people pine for a pro-life Bernie Sanders and flirt anew with baptizing Karl Marx. It includes the lively debate over Rod Dreher's recent book "The Benedict Option," with its insistence that politics cannot save American Christianity and that some form of cultural separatism is essential for religious renewal. And it includes the various Catholic responses to Trump and to the revival of European nationalism — some of which imagine that out of the crisis of Western liberalism a new or different integralism, a more fully Catholic politics, might eventually be born.

Meanwhile Rome, and specifically the men around Pope Francis, seem to both misunderstand and fear this new ferment. Both reactions, fear and ignorance, inform a recent essay in the Jesuit magazine La Civiltà Cattolica, written by two papal confidantes, the Jesuit Rev. Antonio Spadaro and the Protestant journalist Marcelo Figueroa, which has generated thousands of words of intra-Catholic argument in the last few weeks.

Their essay is bad but important. Its seems to intend, reasonably enough, to warn against Catholic support for the darker tendencies in Trumpism — the xenophobia and identity politics, the "stigmatization of enemies," the crude view of Islam and a wider "panorama of threats," the prosperity-gospel inflected worship of success.

But the authors' understanding of American religion seems to start and end with Google searches and anti-evangelical tracts, and their intended attack on Trumpery expands and expands, conflating very different political and religious tendencies, indulging in paranoia about obscure theocratic Protestants and fringe Catholic websites, and ultimately critiquing every kind of American religious conservatism — including the largely anti-political Benedict Option and the pro-life activism fulsomely supported by Francis' papal predecessors — as dangerously illiberal, "theopolitical," Islamic State-esque, "Manichaean," a return to the old integralism that the church no longer supports.

None of this makes any sense. The post-1970s evangelical-Catholic alliance has been flawed in various ways, but it is neither theocratic nor illiberal; if Charles Colson and Richard John Neuhaus were integralists, I am a lemur. The religious right stands in a complex continuity with previous religious reform movements in American history, from abolition to the Social Gospel to Prohibition to civil rights and peace movements in the 1960s. And in its specifically Catholic form, religious conservatism has aspired to exactly the kind of Catholic engagement in liberal-democratic politics anticipated by Leo XIII's "ralliement" and endorsed by the Second Vatican Council.

What Spadaro and Figueroa do not grasp is that the tendencies that they see at work in American Catholicism, the religious votes for the cheerfully pagan Trump and the growing interest in traditionalism, radicalism and separatism, are not the culmination of the Catholic-evangelical alliance but rather a reaction to its political and cultural failures — and the failures of liberal religious politics as well.

In increasing numbers, American Catholics (and Protestants) feel that their leaders and thinkers have spent decades rallying to the republic, trying to bring about its moral and political renewal ... only to see republican virtues decaying, liberalism turning hostile to religious faith, and democratic capitalism delivering disappointment and dislocation. So some of them are reaching backward and sideways or ahead, trying to claim Trumpism or socialism or grasp some as-yet-unknown idea, because they sense that the present order might someday soon be itself an ancien regime from which their religion must slip free.

They may be wrong about this, but their sense of things is shared in certain ways by Pope Francis himself, who has a Trumpish, populist streak in his own right, and whose critiques of the West's technocratic order are notable and pungent. Which is the other bizarre thing about Spadaro and Figueroa's broad brush: As the American Catholic writer Patrick Smith points out, by warning against a Catholicism that takes political sides or indulges in moralistic rhetoric or otherwise declaims on "who is right and who is wrong" in contemporary debates, the pope's men are effectively condemning not only

American conservative Catholics but also the pope's own writings on poverty and environmentalism, his support for grass-roots "popular movements" in the developing world and his stress on the organic link between family, society, religion and the state.

This they surely do not mean to do. But it is precisely this tension, between the Spadaro-Figueroa critique of American religious conservatives and Pope Francis' sometimes harsh assessment of the liberal West, that makes the essay important as well as incoherent — because it reveals something significant about the dilemmas of the Vatican in a populist moment, in which the future of Western politics seems unusually uncertain.

Between Leo XIII and the Second Vatican Council, Rome gradually made its peace with secular and liberal government, and embraced a style of Catholic politics that worked comfortably within the liberal order, rather than against its grain. And the church has good prudential reasons not to lean in too far to any kind of populism or post-liberalism, lest it lead toward authoritarianism or simple disaster.

At the same time the church is supposed to be larger than any particular political philosophy, ready to outlast any particular order and capable of speaking prophetically in periods of transition. It could not remain bound to French monarchists forever; there may come a moment when it cannot remain with whatever liberalism might become.

Again, in the rhetoric of Francis as well as the unsettlement of American Catholics you can see hints that such a moment may be on its way. But in his advisers' essay, in their evident paranoia about what the Americans are up to, you see a different spirit: a fear of novelty and disruption, and a desire for a church that's primarily a steward of social peace, a mild and ecumenical presence, a moderate pillar of the establishment in a stable and permanently liberal age.

At the very least the men in the Vatican who yearn for such a church need to do a better job grasping why so many of their flock, in Europe and the United States, find this vision insufficient to the times.

And then beyond that they might consider the possibility that as in the 19th century, American Catholics, in all their present confusion and occasional extremism, might be closer to grasping what our strange future holds for Catholic politics than Rome.

ROSS DOUTHAT is an Op-Ed columnist for The New York Times.

Easter Is Calling Me Back to the Church

OPINION | BY MARGARET RENKL | MARCH 25, 2018

NASHVILLE — I went to church on Easter Sunday last year, and never went back. It wasn't a boycott, exactly. It was an inability, week after week, to face the other believers. Still, I'd fully intended to go to Mass on Christmas Eve, but at the very last minute a crisis erupted in my extended family — an all-hands-on-deck kind of crisis — so I changed into my jeans and hung my poinsettia-red blouse back in the closet.

In this house, we have never been Christmas-and-Easter-only Christians. My husband and I grew up in the church and raised our children there. Even during the hardest years, when mobilizing three young sons and various configurations of elderly parents felt like running the Iditarod every Sunday morning — even then, we didn't miss Mass.

BARTON SILVERMAN/THE NEW YORK TIMES

Inside St. Patrick's Cathedral during 11 o'clock Mass on Christmas morning, Dec. 25, 1971.

But the 2016 presidential election changed all that for me. I just couldn't forgive my fellow Christians for electing a man who exploited his employees, boasted about his sexual assaults, encouraged violence against citizens who disagreed with him, mocked the disabled and welcomed the support of virulent white supremacists. This is what Jesus meant when he told his followers to love one another?

At church, all I could think about were the millions of people likely to lose their health insurance thanks to Catholic bishops who opposed the birth control mandate in the Affordable Care Act. I was supposed to be thinking about the infinite love of a merciful God, but all I could hear were thousands of Christians shouting, "Build that wall!" By the time Easter had come and gone, I was gone too.

In some ways, there was nothing surprising about this breach. I love my parish, but I have always had a vexed relationship with the church. Long before 2016, the fault line was there, rumbling with every papal pronouncement affirming the male-only priesthood or claiming to speak with moral authority on issues of human sexuality. What kind of faith community denies a sacrament to parishioners who don't happen to have been born heterosexual?

During college and graduate school, I tried to talk myself out of believing in God. The reasons not to believe were multifarious and convincing. The reasons to believe came down to only one: I couldn't not believe. I seem to have been born with a constant ache for the sacred, a deep-rooted need to offer thanks, to ask for help, to sing out in fathomless praise to something. In time I found my way back to God, the most familiar and fundamental something I knew, even if by then my conception of the divine had enlarged beyond any church's ability to define or contain it.

A church isn't a necessary thing to a believer for whom the whole world is holy. But when our first baby was on the way, my husband and I signed on. We could have chosen another branch of Christianity, one whose secular framework more closely matched our own understanding of a church's role in the world. But to a soul imprinted from birth on

Roman Catholicism's stained glass and incense and 2,000 years of art and music, all the other churches just seemed a little slight somehow. Not quite finished.

And if all human institutions are by definition imperfect, why not throw in your lot with the one that made you, the one where everyone you love belongs? The worldly church is always a work in progress, and there is still hope for its redemption. "Anyway," my husband said, "if a priest doesn't baptize this baby, you know my mother will just take him into the bathroom and baptize him herself."

In the past year, while my husband and his father were at church on Sunday mornings, I was in the woods, where God has always seemed more palpably present to me anyway. (And not just to me: "Some keep the Sabbath going to Church," Emily Dickinson wrote back in the 19th century. "I keep it, staying at Home.") For me, a church can't summon half the awe and gratitude inspired by a full-throated forest in all its indifferent splendor.

The year away from church hasn't made me miss the place itself. I don't miss the stained glass. I don't miss the gleaming chalice or the glowing candles or the sweeping vestments. But I do miss being part of a congregation. I miss standing side by side with other people, our eyes gazing in the same direction, our voices murmuring the same prayers in a fallen world. I miss the wiggling babies grinning at me over their parents' shoulders. I miss reaching for a stranger to offer the handshake of peace. I miss the singing.

So I will be at Mass again on Easter morning, as I have been on almost every Easter morning of my life. I will wear white and remember the ones I loved who sat beside me in the pew and whose participation in the eternal has found another form, whatever it turns out to be. I will lift my voice in song and give thanks for my life. I will pray for my church and my country, especially the people my church and my country are failing. And then I will walk into the world and do my best to practice resurrection.

MARGARET RENKL is a contributing opinion writer.

‘God Made You This Way,’ Pope Is Said to Have Told Gay Man

BY JASON HOROWITZ | MAY 21, 2018

ROME — A Chilean survivor of clerical sex abuse has said that Pope Francis told him in a private meeting this month that God had made him gay and that both God and the pontiff loved him that way, a remarkable expression of inclusion for the leader of the Roman Catholic Church.

“He said to me, ‘Juan Carlos, that’s not a problem,’ ” said Juan Carlos Cruz, the abuse survivor, describing having told the pope he was gay in a long meeting in the Vatican. “You have to be happy with who you are. God made you this way and loves you this way, and the pope loves you this way.”

The Vatican declined to comment on the pope’s private remarks.

Mr. Cruz had already said that Francis had apologized in the meeting for the large-scale sexual abuse scandal involving Chilean clergy members, but over the weekend, he also told the Spanish newspaper El País about the pope’s remarks about his homosexuality. In a separate interview Sunday night, Mr. Cruz, through tears, explained that he had told Francis in their nearly three-hour private meeting that he had maintained his Catholic faith even though Chilean bishops had apparently told the pope that he had left the church “for a life of perversion.”

In July 2013, the pope responded to questions about a supposed “gay lobby” in the Vatican by saying “Who am I to judge,” a remark that caused celebration among liberals and consternation among conservatives. His reported remarks to Mr. Cruz added to the debate over whether Francis believes homosexuality is a choice.

Vatican officials, however, cautioned against interpreting the pontiff’s pastoral outreach as a definitive ruling on the nature-versus-nurture question or as a change in church teaching.

The Catechism of the Catholic Church states that people with "homosexual tendencies" "must be accepted with respect, compassion, and sensitivity," but it also calls a "deep-seated" homosexual inclination and its acts "intrinsically disordered" and "contrary to the natural law."

The pope's remarks, if accurate, would reinforce his vision of inclusion, accompaniment and mercy. It is an emphasis that is increasingly evident throughout a church hierarchy that he is reshaping.

Archbishop Matteo Maria Zuppi of Bologna, sometimes called the "Bergoglio of Italy" for his similarity to Francis, the former Jorge Mario Bergoglio, published on Monday a preface to the Italian version of "Building a Bridge," a book by the American Jesuit priest James Martin about reaching out to gay Catholics.

"The intent of the book is to help pastors develop an attitude of understanding, as well as a capacity for accompaniment, towards their homosexual brothers and sisters," the archbishop writes.

The pope has been increasingly assertive over the spring, five years into his papacy, especially after he seemed hobbled by missteps on the Chilean sexual abuse scandal.

He announced on Saturday that Óscar Romero, a Salvadoran bishop shot and killed by right-wing forces for preaching against military oppression and American meddling, would be canonized in October.

The next day, he reshaped the College of Cardinals, which will choose his successor. He surprisingly named 14 new cardinals, 11 of whom are under 80 and thus able to vote in the next conclave.

After the appointment in June of the new cardinals, who come from across the world, Francis will have named 59, or nearly half of the 125 voting cardinals. Pope Benedict XVI, a conservative who retired in 2013, named 47 of the remaining electors. And Pope John Paul II, also a conservative, elevated 19.

And the Vatican issued a major document last week on economic ethics that insisted that profit for profits' sake was "illegitimate" and an "amoral culture of waste," reflecting Francis' fierce criticism of the inequality caused by capitalism.

But it was the pope's muscular response to the Chilean sexual abuse scandal, which seemed months ago to hold the potential of tarnishing his entire pontificate, that has been most remarkable.

During a trip to Chile this year, the pope repeatedly defended a Chilean bishop against accusations of a cover-up. Francis called the claims of abuse survivors "calumny."

The resulting backlash forced him to send the Vatican's top sex-crimes investigator to Chile. He returned with a scathing, 2,300-page report that suggested that bishops there had misled the pope and destroyed records to prevent the public from learning that abusive priests had been moved from diocese to diocese. Francis said the systemic failures had left him "perplexed and ashamed."

The pope convoked all Chilean bishops to Rome for days of intense meetings, at the conclusion of which all 34 offered their resignation, a first. They begged forgiveness for the "pain they caused the victims, the pope, the people of God, and our country for the grave errors and omissions we committed."

The pope is yet to accept their resignations, but he is expected to start with Bishop Juan Barros Madrid, whom he had repeatedly defended.

In a letter to the bishops, Francis said that merely removing the bishops would be insufficient. "It would be a serious omission on our part not to delve into the roots," he wrote.

Francis' meeting with the bishops followed his personal meetings two weeks ago with the survivors of abuse whom he had previously accused of slander. According to Mr. Cruz, Francis was decidedly on the side of the victims and entirely welcoming of the Chilean's sexual orientation.

Mr. Cruz said that his lawyer warned him in 2009 that the church would focus on his homosexuality, leaving him vulnerable and threatening to make life extremely difficult for him.

He said that his lawyer later told him that Cardinal Francisco Javier Errázuriz, a confidant of Francis, had raised the question of whether Mr. Cruz could even be considered a victim because, Mr. Cruz said, "I was gay and I might have liked it."

"It was horrible," he added. "This has always weighed on me."

In his meeting with Francis on a Sunday at his Santa Marta residence, Mr. Cruz said he had told the pope that he was worried he would think less of him. Mr. Cruz acknowledged that he was gay and, jokingly, not the reincarnation of Saint Aloysius Gonzaga, a model of the virtue of purity, but someone who tried to be "a good person."

It was then that the pope reassured him, he said. The two went on to chat about Mr. Cruz's personal life, his not having a partner, and his relationship with his family.

Mr. Cruz also told the pope of his "most wonderful friends, who are also Catholic and who struggle with this."

In the interview, Mr. Cruz said that since the article in El País was published over the weekend, some of those gay Catholic friends had written to him saying of the pope, "Did he really tell you that? I feel so relieved." Another wrote, "I'm in the gym and I feel like crying."

Mr. Cruz said he wanted to reveal the pope's remarks because "people have to know this man like he really is."

"He is a loving man who really embraces everybody," he said.

Can the Catholic Church 'Evolve' on L.G.B.T. Rights?

OPINION | BY JOHN GEHRING | JULY 5, 2018

A GROWING NUMBER of Americans now broadly support equal rights for gay, lesbian and transgender people. It's tempting to view this as inevitable, but less than a decade ago many Democrats, including Barack Obama, didn't even publicly support same-sex marriage. The speed at which L.G.B.T. rights became a mainstream issue, including for many religious denominations, represents nothing less than a dizzying cultural transformation.

What does this revolution mean for the Catholic Church, an ancient institution that thinks in centuries, and holds a view of human sexuality at odds with the shifting cultural winds?

Well, last week, the Vatican used "L.G.B.T." for what is believed to be the first time ever in a document prepared for a major gathering of bishops and young people in October. "Some L.G.B.T. youth," it reads, want to "benefit from greater closeness and experience greater care from the church." The document also acknowledges that many young Catholics disagree with the church's teaching on same-sex marriage.

Not exactly breaking news, you might argue. But adopting "L.G.B.T." is emblematic of an emerging shift in the church's posture toward gay, lesbian and transgender people. Catholic teaching documents have typically used "homosexual" or referred to those with "homosexual tendencies," which reduce a person's multidimensional humanity to the mechanics of sex. Using the L.G.B.T. descriptor, often preferred by many gay, lesbian and transgender people, is a sign of respect.

Pope Francis has opened space for a deeper, more authentic conversation about how the church can keep one foot planted in Catholic tradition without being afraid to step into the lived experiences of others. When Pope Francis gave the most famous papal sound bite in history five years ago — "Who am I to judge?" — even his colloquial use of the word "gay" caused a stir in traditional Catholic circles. While the pope has strongly defended church teaching on marriage as exclusively between a man and a woman, he prioritizes listening and personal encounter over finger-wagging denunciations. He's met with transgender people, and when he spoke privately last month with a Chilean clergy sexual abuse survivor, the pope told him that God made him gay and loved him.

There are other signs of progress. The prominent Jesuit priest and author Rev. James Martin, who has been banned from speaking at some Catholic institutions in the United States simply for encouraging the church to build bridges with L.G.B.T. people, was recently invited to give a keynote address at the Vatican-sponsored World Meeting of Families in Dublin later this summer. At the last gathering in Philadelphia three years ago, the only discussion about L.G.B.T. issues came from celibate gay Catholics who spoke about chastity.

The pope's emphasis on encounter and engagement is trickling down to influence other church leaders. Cardinal Joe Tobin of Newark welcomed a pilgrimage of L.G.B.T. Catholics to the city's cathedral last spring. In this month's issue of U.S. Catholic magazine, a deacon in the diocese of St. Petersburg, Fla., wrote movingly about his transgender daughter, and challenged the church's notion of "gender ideology," a term that has been used to discredit the push for transgender rights.

Despite this progress, the Catholic Church must do far more not only to acknowledge the humanity of L.G.B.T. people, but also to recognize most want the same committed, loving relationships as straight couples. After the Supreme Court's 2015 decision legalizing same-sex marriage, Cardinal Blase Cupich of Chicago called for "real, not rhetorical" respect for gays and lesbians. The court decision, which he opposed, still offered an opportunity for "mature and serene reflections," the cardinal wrote.

Catholic leaders in the United States should consider studying a proposal made by Bishop Franz-Josef Bode, the vice president of the German bishops' conference, who has encouraged a thoughtful discussion on whether Catholic clergymen might offer a type of blessing for Catholics in same-sex relationships. “Although ‘marriage for all’ differs clearly from the church’s concept of marriage, it’s now political reality,” the bishop said. “We have to ask ourselves how we’re encountering those who form such relationships, and are also involved in the church, how we’re accompanying them pastorally and liturgically.”

The church’s own language toward L.G.B.T. people is a stumbling block to its professed commitment to human dignity. While the Catholic catechism, which details church teaching, forbids any violence or “unjust discrimination” toward people who are gay or lesbian, it also describes sexual intimacy between them as “intrinsically disordered.” Before he became pope, Cardinal Joseph Ratzinger wrote in 1986 that homosexuality represents a “strong tendency ordered toward an intrinsic moral evil.”

Many L.G.B.T. Catholics are also forced to live in what the Rev. Bryan Massingale, a Fordham University theologian, calls “the open closet.” This is particularly true at Catholic schools, where in recent years more than 70 L.G.B.T. church employees and Catholic schoolteachers have been fired or lost their jobs in employment disputes. L.G.B.T. Catholic employees have their lives subjected to moral scrutiny in ways heterosexual Catholics never do. Straight Catholics are not fired for using contraception, for example, or having sex before marriage. Why not judge Catholics for not welcoming immigrants, feeding the hungry or visiting the sick? In the Gospel of Matthew, failing to do that earns you a ticket to damnation.

Five years into the Francis papacy, a pope who emphasizes mercy and strikes a more welcoming tone toward L.G.B.T. people is helping to rescue the church from a culture-war Christianity that drives people away. But until the Catholic hierarchy can find more tangible ways to institutionalize a commitment to the rights of gay, lesbian and transgender people, the exodus of Catholics will continue. Surveys show most Catholics support same-sex marriage, and the church’s opposition to L.G.B.T. rights drives young people away.

Those who are raised Catholic are more likely than those raised in any other religion to cite negative religious treatment of gay and lesbian people as the primary reason they leave, according to the nonpartisan Public Religion Research Institute. Firing L.G.B.T. Catholics and using degrading language such as "intrinsically disordered" erode the church's credibility to speak about justice, love and human dignity.

If the first step toward change is listening, Bishop John Stowe of Lexington, Ky., had it right when he addressed a national gathering of L.G.B.T. Catholics last year. "In a church that has not always valued or welcomed your presence, we need to hear your voices and take seriously your experiences," he said.

It's time to make sure that is more than just an applause line.

JOHN GEHRING is Catholic program director at Faith in Public Life and author of "The Francis Effect: A Radical Pope's Challenge to the American Catholic Church."

CHAPTER 4

The Pope as International Actor

A witness to conflict at home in Latin America, Pope Francis has taken a strong interest in global affairs. Expanding the Vatican's role abroad, Francis has devoted several state visits to addressing climate change, sectarian conflict and the rise of nationalist populism. However, critics have also observed other motives in Francis' public diplomacy: rehabilitating the negative image of the church and recruiting new congregants in the developing world. As European church membership continues to decline, Francis has turned to Africa and Asia for new converts.

Prayer Meeting Shows Pope's Larger Vision

BY JIM YARDLEY | JUNE 6, 2014

VATICAN CITY — From the earliest days of his papacy, when he walked slowly into a grand reception hall in the Apostolic Palace for his first meeting with a curious diplomatic corps, Pope Francis has promoted a fairly conventional foreign policy agenda: fight poverty, pursue peace, bridge ecumenical or interreligious divisions and protect the environment.

What has been unconventional is how Francis has elevated that agenda through adroitly timed gestures and initiatives — none more unexpected than the prayer summit meeting that he is holding on Sunday with the presidents of Israel and the Palestinian Authority.

He has placed himself in perhaps the world's most complex diplomatic dispute — at a moment when American-led negotiations have collapsed — by arguing that dialogue and prayer can help.

If few analysts expect any major breakthroughs, Francis' summit meeting shows how he is trying to pursue his goals by positioning the Vatican as an independent, global diplomatic player. Analysts also note that Francis' status as the first Latin American pope has given him credibility in the non-Western world and is helping the Vatican have influence on a broader array of issues and disputes.

"He is planning his own global role," said Alberto Melloni, a Vatican historian. "He is showing there is a space in international relations for a different diplomacy. That is the purpose of this diplomatic action — to show they are independent and reliable for the world."

Centuries ago, popes dominated global affairs, starting wars or ending them, exercising enormous influence in Europe and adjudicating between European powers as they expanded their colonial empires into Africa and the Americas. Papal influence was much more limited during the last century, with popes trying and failing to end both world wars. The most notable exception was Pope John Paul II, who is credited for his role in the collapse of Communism in Eastern Europe.

When Francis became pope in March 2013, the historic nature of his papacy was framed largely in the context of the evolution of the Roman Catholic Church. Having an Argentine pope signaled that the Catholic center of gravity had shifted from Europe, where membership was stagnant, to Latin America and the global south, where it was expanding.

But Francis has since shown that his biography and popular personal style have also influenced how the Vatican engages on global political issues. He is hardly the first pope to speak out against poverty and inequality. Yet his work in the slums of Buenos Aires has lent him extra credibility, as has his status as a product of the developing world.

His first papal trip was to the Italian island of Lampedusa to draw attention to human trafficking and the global indifference to the thousands of refugees trying to reach Europe, with many dying in the Mediterranean. Global headlines also followed when he wrote a mildly scolding letter in January to the political and economic elites of the World Economic Forum in Davos, Switzerland, in which he decried global hunger as "intolerable."

Francis has spoken often about his concerns over the fate of Christians in the Middle East, and he has used this issue, as well as his broader nonviolence agenda, to insert the Vatican into diplomacy in the region. Last September, he staged a huge prayer vigil at St. Peter's Square as the United States and other Western powers were contemplating strikes against Syria.

The pope extended his invitation for Sunday's prayer meeting during a visit last month to Israel, Jordan and the West Bank — and apparently it surprised almost everyone, underscoring the unpredictability that sometimes informs his approach. One of the most resonant moments of his trip came when he made an unscheduled stop to pray beside a security barrier that Israel had erected in Jerusalem.

To some, it is surprising that a Latin American pontiff who has traveled relatively little outside his home region would so assertively involve himself in the Middle East. But others note that the Vatican has played an active role in Latin American politics for decades, including mediating a dispute in the late 1970s between Argentina and Chile over rights to the Beagle Channel.

"In Latin America, the idea of papal intervention is a natural thing to think about," said Philip Jenkins, a history professor with the Institute for Studies of Religion at Baylor University.

Vatican officials have emphasized that the pope is not planning to try to mediate specific disputes between the two sides on Sunday. Delegations led by Presidents Shimon Peres of Israel and Mahmoud Abbas of the Palestinian Authority will join Francis on Sunday evening in the Vatican gardens for a program of Jewish, Muslim and Christian prayers, as well as music. "No one presumes that peace will break out Monday," the Rev. Pierbattista Pizzaballa, who is involved in planning for the prayer meeting and is the custodian of Catholic properties in the Holy Land, said at a news conference at the Vatican on Friday. "The intent is to recreate the desire, the possibility, the dream — to reopen a door that had been closed for some time."

ELISABETTA POVOLEDO contributed reporting.

Tracing the Roots of Pope Francis' Climate Plans for 2015

OPINION | BY ANDREW C. REVKIN | DEC. 31, 2014

ONE OF THE HIGHLIGHTS of my year, perhaps my career, was being able to participate in "Sustainable Humanity, Sustainable Nature: Our Responsibility," a four-day Vatican workshop aimed at shaping strategies for human advancement that are attuned to the planet's limits, organized by the Pontifical Academy of Sciences and Academy of Social Sciences last May.

Now there are signs that the themes and conclusions developed in those sessions are helping to shape Pope Francis' planned push for serious international commitments in 2015 to curb greenhouse gases and gird communities, particularly the poorest, against climate-related hazards.

A first step will come in less than three weeks, when, during his visit to the Philippines, the pope is scheduled to have lunch with some survivors of the typhoon that devastated Tacloban in 2012. The scope of the human calamity there was as much a result of deep poverty and poorly governed urban growth as the ferocity of Typhoon Haiyan.

The social and environmental roots of that disaster provide just the context the Vatican needs to reinforce its case that sustainable human progress will come as much through attacking poverty and fostering fairness as boosting environmental protection.

Those twin themes resonated throughout the Vatican meeting and have built since then, particularly in a speech delivered in London on Nov. 7 by Bishop Marcelo Sánchez Sorondo, who, as chancellor of both pontifical academies, was the chief organizer of the Vatican sustainability workshop.

That speech sketches out much of the pope's plans on climate change for the coming year. (You probably saw John Vidal's article on the pope's climate plans in the Guardian last Saturday, or the heaps of coverage that followed, but if you dig in a bit, you'll see that nearly every point in the story came from Sorondo's lecture.)

In the speech, Sorondo carefully placed Francis' steps in the broader context of Vatican actions going back to Pope Paul VI in 1975. Here are some excerpts:

The basics:

> *Today solid scientific evidence exists that global climate is changing and that human activity based on the use of fossil materials contributes decisively to this trend. Coupled with an economy based on profit and on the games finance plays in order to profit from money itself, without a clear orientation to the production of goods, this leads to social exclusion and the new forms of slavery such as forced labour, prostitution, organ trafficking, and the use of drugs as a method of corruption. Therefore, a program in the light of the Populorum progressio and Pope Montini's further interpretations must include climate stabilization, the sustainable development of the natural environment and social inclusion focused on the centrality of the human being and the common good.*

On the obligations that attend the Anthropocene:

> *[J]ust as humanity confronted "revolutionary change" (Rerum Novarum) in the 19th century at the time of Industrialization, today we have changed the natural environment so much that scientists, using a word coined by our Academy, tend to define our era as the Anthropocene, that is to say, a period of time in which human action is having a decisive impact on the planet due to the use of fossil fuels. If current trends continue, this century will witness unprecedented climate change and the destruction of the ecosystem, with tragic consequences for us all.*
>
> *Human action that doesn't respect nature has a boomerang effect on human beings, creating inequality and increasing what Pope Francis has defined as "globalisation of indifference" and "economics of exclusion" (Evangelii Gaudium), which endanger solidarity and present and future generations.*

On the world's wealth and energy gaps:

> *Advances in measured productivity in all sectors — agriculture, industry and services — enable us to imagine an end to poverty, shared*

prosperity, and a further increase in life expectancy. However, unjust social structures (Evangelii Gaudium) have become an obstacle to the appropriate and sustainable organization of production and to the equitable distribution of its fruits, which are both necessary to achieve those objectives. …

For example, 50 percent of the available energy is used by less than a billion people, whereas its negative impacts on the environmental affect three billion people who do not have access to it. These three billion people, in fact, have so little access to modern energy that they are forced to cook, heat and light their homes using methods harmful to their health.

A warning, but also "a message of hope and joy":

Today we need to establish a mutually beneficial relationship: the economy needs to be imbued with true values, and respect for God's creation should promote human dignity and well being.

On these issues, all religions and all people of good will can agree. Today's young people will embrace them to create a better world. The message of the Pontifical Academies is an urgent warning because the dangers of the Anthropocene are real and the injustice of the globalization of indifference is a serious issue. Yet, our message is also one of hope and joy. This is exactly what the Blessed Pope Paul VI wanted to achieve with his project of the civilization of love: a healthier, safer, fairer, more prosperous and more sustainable world is within our reach. The believers among us ask the Lord to give us our daily bread as food for the body and soul.

The papal game plan, including a possible encyclical and a meeting of all faiths this year:

Following the lead of the great recent Popes, especially Paul VI, Pope Francis has a unique role as a religious leader and moral guidance to protect, preserve, sustainably develop the natural environment and achieve that social inclusion that can no longer be postponed. The problem of climate change has become a major social and moral problem, and mentalities can only be changed on moral and religious grounds.

Therefore, our Academics supported the Pope's initiative to publish an Encyclical or another such important document on climate and social inclusion to influence next year's crucial decisions.

In fact, the idea is to convene a meeting with the religious leaders of the main religions to make all people aware of the state of our climate and the tragedy of social exclusion starting from the biblical message that man is the steward of nature and of its environmental and human development according to its potential and not against it, as Paul IV intended.

Thus, the prophetic message of Paul VI continues to be valid even in this new era that humanity is beginning. It is connected to the programmatic expression that he used at the end of the 1975 Jubilee Year, when he urged everyone to promote "the civilization of love" as its successful culmination. In terms of public and social life, and relationship with nature, this civilization of love is the coronation of the period of grace and good will of the Second Vatican Council, or rather the beginning of a new era of grace and good will, which history unfolds before us.

I encourage you to read the full speech on the website of The Tablet, a weekly Catholic magazine.

I smiled when I read that last section about the prospect of a "civilization of love." The other central theme permeating Sorondo's talk — and the meeting last May — was the role of values, more than data, in shaping humanity's choices.

Here's how I described this theme in the summation I delivered on the final day at the Vatican:

It says much that even some of the most accomplished scientists at this meeting articulated that progress on climate, energy, equity, education and conservation of living resources will be driven by values and faith more than data and predictive models.

In a discussion over dinner, Walter Munk, at 96 one of great oceanographers of modern times, spoke not of gigatons of carbon or megawatts of electricity: "This requires a miracle of love and unselfishness," he said.

Almost all you need is love. Here's to Pope Francis, and Walter Munk.

Update, Jan. 1, 2015, 8:49 a.m. | Chris Mooney's broader reflection on Pope Francis, Catholicism and science is an essential read: "Our new pro-science pontiff: Pope Francis on climate change, evolution, and the Big Bang."

Update, Jan. 2, 9:10 p.m. | Alexander Lucie-Smith, a Catholic priest, doctor of moral theology and consulting editor of The Catholic Herald in Britain has written a very interesting piece questioning the need for an encyclical from Pope Francis. He notes that the church has long been pressing for care of the environment, but warns that global warming poses particularly complicated questions related to "proportionate benefit":

> *The ethical principles are not in doubt. It is wrong, for example, to destroy nature without a proportionate reason. Everyone knows that. What constitutes proportionate reason is something that ethicists and scientists need to work out between them. If, for example one is to build a dam, that is certainly an interference in nature and a destruction of a natural environment — but is it worth it? Will the dam bring some proportionate benefit? That in itself is hard to determine. When I was schoolboy we did projects on the Aswan High Dam, which was seen as a towering human achievement back in the seventies. But would it ever have got built today? Our understanding of the usefulness or otherwise of dams has changed, and will continue to do so over time. Look at the Three Gorges Dam in China, a project that has been damned by virtually everyone. I suspect that forty years ago the consensus would have been very different.*

ANDREW C. REVKIN created the Dot Earth blog at The New York Times to explore ways to balance human needs and the planet's limits.

Pope Francis, in New York, Takes On Extremism and Inequality

BY MICHAEL WILSON | SEPT. 25, 2015

BY MOTORCADE AND POPEMOBILE and simple shoe leather, in a daylong tour up and down Manhattan that found pockets of joy and pain, wealth and want, Pope Francis on Friday called for social justice and peace in addresses to world leaders and workaday New Yorkers alike. He ended with a stirring homily that was both an ode to the city and a reminder to watch for glimpses of the presence of God among the poorest of the poor.

"In big cities, beneath the roar of traffic, beneath the rapid pace of change, so many faces pass by unnoticed because they have no 'right' to be there, no right to be part of the city," Francis said in a Mass before 20,000 at Madison Square Garden. "They are the foreigners, the children who go without schooling, those deprived of medical insurance, the homeless, the forgotten elderly. These people stand at the edges of our great avenues, in our streets, in deafening anonymity."

That theme, that "God is living in our cities," provided an apt conclusion to a day spent navigating New York's complicated fabric of rich and struggling. It was the pope's first visit to the city, where the longtime hum of the machines of commerce and prosperity has brought the very excesses he has spent his papacy pushing against. It was impossible to ignore, behind the rows and rows of well-wishers who packed Central Park's broad meadow, the soaring columns of skyscrapers with penthouses that are home to many of the world's wealthiest people.

He spoke of that divide often during the day, from his first remarks before the United Nations General Assembly, where he called for respect for "those considered disposable because they are only considered as part of a statistic," to his closing homily's observation that "big cities also conceal the faces of all those people who don't appear to belong, or are second-class citizens."

ERIC THAYER FOR THE NEW YORK TIMES

Before stepping inside the school, Francis walked along a security gate, greeting well-wishers.

Francis sought out some of those faces on a day of grand pageantry and small gestures that brought him before the relatives of the fallen at the footprints of the twin towers and, hours later, the upturned smiles of East Harlem schoolchildren not yet born the day those buildings were destroyed.

Perhaps the day's greatest spectacle was his winding sweep through a swath of Central Park, a logistical feat that included screening tens of thousands of ticketholders, one bag at a time. The throngs roared their greetings to the "people's pope," using the name by which he is commonly known: "Viva Papa!"

In spite of the tight ring of dark-suited security that surrounded the pope at all times, many were allowed a closer look. Among them: a New York police officer, Terrance McGhee, in a wheelchair at the World Trade Center site, whom Francis stooped to greet; dozens of children outside Our Lady Queen of Angels in East Harlem, who waved cellphones as Francis gave head-pats and high-fives; the day laborer at the Garden Mass, a medal under his shirt of St. Jude, the patron saint of lost causes; the babies held out for a blessing in the Garden.

Just after 8 on the crisp early autumn morning, Francis left his papal apartment on the Upper East Side for his address to the General Assembly, the fifth by a pope and the first for him. He called for environmental responsibility and lamented the impact of decades of abuse on the world's poor.

"They are cast off by society, forced to live off what is discarded and suffer unjustly from the consequences of abuse of the environment," Francis said. "These phenomena are part of today's widespread and quietly growing 'culture of waste.' "

From there, the layers of political commentary that followed his remarks in Washington earlier in the week seemed to fall away, leaving the day one of pure emotion for Francis and those wishing to be near him.

It was also a respite from nagging thoughts that society's ills will remain after he has left New York, the middle leg of a United States visit that began in the capital and ends on Sunday.

From the United Nations, the pope's motorcade sped downtown to the World Trade Center site. Upon arriving, he walked into the September 11 Memorial and Museum, flanked by Cardinal Timothy M. Dolan and others, slowly making his way past the bottom of the memorial's North Pool to the top of the South Pool.

There, he paused for a long moment of silent reflection, gazing down into the pool of cascading water, which, from the visitor's vantage point, has no visible bottom. He looked at the names of the victims on the panel at his fingertips, one of many panels at the site that, together, bear thousands of names: Boyle, Woods, Nguyen, Lynch. The falling water brought the only sound. He and Cardinal Dolan each left a white rose on the panel.

Francis turned at that point, meeting a long line of relatives who shared memories of those who had died on Sept. 11. He listened, often clutching an outstretched hand, and once patting a little girl's head. He entered the museum and its Foundation Hall, where a multifaith ceremony of striking breadth — representatives of Judaism, Islam, Hinduism, Sikhism and Christianity — heard him eulogize those who died trying to rescue others.

"New York City firefighters walked into the crumbling towers, with no concern for their own well-being," he said. "Many succumbed. Their sacrifice enabled great numbers to be saved." He called the site "a place of saved lives, a hymn to the triumph of life over the prophets of destruction and death."

And he called for peace. "Peace in our homes, our families, our schools and communities. Peace in all those places where war never seems to end. Peace for those faces which have known nothing but pain."

The pope walked through the museum, past the relics and totems that have become indelible images from that day 14 years ago, like the

TODD HEISLER/THE NEW YORK TIMES

Pope Francis arriving Friday at the General Assembly of the United Nations. "Every one of these political, juridical and technical advances is a path towards attaining the ideal of human fraternity and a means for its greater realization," he said.

hulking section of the trade center's foundation wall, the "slurry wall," and the "last column," an icon covered with pictures and truck and unit numbers from the city's firehouses and police precincts.

The pope's motorcade then left the memorial. Crowds gathered along his route uptown to his apartment; a woman, tears streaming down her face, hoisted a baby on her shoulders. All day, enormous crowds lined sidewalks behind metal barriers and tall fences, straining for a glimpse of the figure in white.

"I'm Jewish, and this is still the coolest moment of my life," Julie Rodgers, 70, said.

The crowds swelled around Central Park during a break in the papal schedule. There was some jostling and name-calling among the hordes of ticketholders, but the police reported no major disturbances. Scores of people lined up along the sidewalks outside the park, filling block upon block. Some were eventually turned away, crying. Others fainted in the heat.

The afternoon's first stop for Francis was Our Lady Queen of the Angels School on East 112th Street. The neighborhood was perhaps the day's least polished backdrop, with its hair salons and "We Buy Gold" signs. ("I hope he brings some blessings to the block," a local superintendent had said on Thursday.)

Inside a brightly colored classroom, he warmly greeted about two dozen children — "This is nice!" he said — and examined class projects — "This is a solar panel," one boy explained — before evoking the Rev. Dr. Martin Luther King Jr.

"His dream was that many children, many people could have equal opportunities," Francis said. He joked to thc students that he was giving them homework: "Please don't forget to pray for me."

Then he met a group of immigrants, who gave him gifts — a soccer ball, a hard hat, a tool belt.

From there, he went to Central Park, where the crowds were still waiting, stepping into his popemobile to cruise about 12 blocks at a walker's pace, beneath English elms and pin oaks, toward Columbus

Circle. The journey lasted only about 15 minutes, but it exposed the pope to his largest crowd of the day by far.

The Mass at the Garden was celebrated with the choreography of a concert befitting the hall before a rapt audience.

"A hope which liberates us from the forces pushing us to isolation and lack of concern for the lives of others, for the life of our city," Francis said. "A hope which frees us from empty connections, from abstract analyses or sensationalistic routines. A hope which is unafraid of involvement, which acts as a leaven wherever we happen to live and work. A hope which makes us see, even in the midst of smog, the presence of God as he continues to walk the streets of our city."

Reporting was contributed by **AL BAKER**, **NICHOLAS CASEY**, **DAVID W. DUNLAP**, **LISA W. FODERARO**, **SANDRA E. GARCIA**, **DAVID GONZALEZ**, **C. J. HUGHES**, **BENJAMIN MUELLER**, **SHARON OTTERMAN**, **KATE PASTOR**, **NOAH REMNICK**, **LIZ ROBBINS**, **RICK ROJAS**, **MARC SANTORA**, **NATE SCHWEBER**, **KIRK SEMPLE**, **JEFFREY E. SINGER**, **JOHN SURICO** and **REBECCA WHITE**.

How the Vatican Can Shed Light on the Holocaust

OPINION | BY GERALD POSNER | JULY 29, 2016

ON FRIDAY, Pope Francis is to become the third Roman Catholic pope to visit Auschwitz. John Paul II was the first Polish pope in the church's 2,000-year history. Auschwitz is less than an hour from where he was born, and his 1979 visit was poignant. Every bit as dramatic was the 2006 visit by the German-born Benedict XVI who had at 14 been a member of the Hitler Youth.

But Francis' visit could be the most significant ever if he uses the symbolic backdrop to break with the policies of six predecessors over 70 years and order the release of the Vatican's sealed Holocaust-era archives.

The debate over the church's secret wartime files is not new. The Vatican is the only country in Europe that refuses to open all of its World War II archives to independent historians and researchers. The issue is more than simply an academic debate over the appropriate rules for public disclosure of historically significant documents. The church's files are thought to contain important information about the Holocaust in Nazi-occupied Eastern Europe. The Vatican had eyes and ears in the killing fields: tens of thousands of parish priests who sent letters and reports to their bishops, who in turn forwarded them to the secretary of state in Vatican City. One of the monsignors in charge of reviewing those thousands of reports was Giovanni Battista Montini, later Pope Paul VI.

It is little wonder that historians are eager to study the Vatican's Holocaust-era papers. The accounts by the parish priests may help answer lingering questions of when and what the Vatican knew about the Nazi murder machinery. The files are likely to shed light on whether the wartime pope, Pius XII, could have done more to try to stop the Holocaust.

Also buried inside the secret archives are the early records of the

ANTHONY RUSSO

scandal-ridden Vatican Bank, created during World War II. Those documents could resolve conclusively how much business the Vatican did with the Third Reich, as well as the extent of insurance company investments that yielded enormous profits from life insurance policies of Jews sent to Auschwitz, which I uncovered in my own reporting.

And finally, the church's secret files might resolve the debate over whether several postwar refugee-smuggling networks that were run from Rome separately by an Austrian bishop, a German priest and a Croatian priest — and through which Nazi criminals escaped — were freelance operations, or instead parts of a program that had the pope's blessing.

The church has since the 1960s released some wartime files, while refusing unfettered access by historians. In the 1990s, the administration of President Bill Clinton ordered federal agencies to release relevant Holocaust files, and also spearheaded an effort that persuaded several dozen other nations to do the same. The Vatican was an outlier.

The 2013 election of Pope Francis held out the promise for a change in the church's longstanding policy of secrecy. While still the archbishop of Buenos Aires, he had been asked about the dispute over the Holocaust-era files. The Vatican, he answered, "should open them and clarify everything." Many Vaticanologists thought he would use a 2014 visit to Israel to free the files. But Francis did not say anything publicly about the papers on that visit.

Francis last discussed the issue in a November 2014 interview with the Israeli newspaper Yediot Ahronot. The pope asked: "Did Pius XII remain silent in the face of the extermination of the Jews? Did he say all he should have said? We will have to open the archives to know exactly what happened." According to Francis: "There is an agreement between the Vatican and Italy from 1929 that prevents us from opening the archives to researchers at this point in time. But because of the time that has passed since World War II, I see no problem with opening the archives the moment we sort out the legal and bureaucratic matters."

The 1929 agreement Francis cited is the Lateran Pacts between the Vatican and Benito Mussolini's Fascist Italy. It gave the church full sovereignty over Vatican City. The agreement declared that the pope was not only the equivalent of a secular monarch but also endowed with divine rights. Instead of preventing the church from releasing its archives, as Francis suggested, the agreement invests the Vatican with inviolable powers to set its own policies independent of any interference from Italy. All that is required to open the long-sealed archives is a papal decree.

Jewish advocacy groups, human rights organizations and concentration camp survivors hope that Francis' commitment to reform will trump the desire of Vatican traditionalists to keep the documents buried forever. On the very grounds where the Nazis murdered more than a million victims, most of them Jews, Pope Francis can do much more than have a photo opportunity and offer a generic condemnation of the depths of human depravity. By freeing the Vatican's Holocaust-era files he will pay a singular and lasting tribute to the dead.

GERALD POSNER is the author, most recently, of "God's Bankers: A History of Money and Power at the Vatican."

Balancing Act for Pope in Egypt: Outreach to Muslims, and Speaking Out for Christians

BY JASON HOROWITZ | APRIL 27, 2017

POPE FRANCIS DEPARTED from his prepared remarks at a special prayer service honoring Christian martyrs in Rome last weekend to tell the story of a Muslim man who watched Islamist terrorists cut the throat of his Christian wife because she refused to discard her crucifix.

"He, Muslim, had this cross of pain that he bore without rancor," the pope said, his voice filled with emotion. "He sought refuge in the love of his wife, graced by martyrdom."

That anecdote — balancing the brutal murder of a Christian by Islamist militants with a Muslim's love for his wife — serves as a preview of the pope's message when he visits Egypt on Friday.

Francis is expected to highlight the plight of Christians amid recent violence in Egypt, while continuing his mission to reach out to Muslims. Even for a politically savvy pope, that is a delicate balancing act, on top of obvious security concerns in a country recently attacked by the Islamic State. Palm Sunday bombings of two Christian churches killed more than 40 people, nearly killed the head of the Coptic Church and prompted President Abdel Fattah el-Sisi to declare a three-month state of emergency.

Francis will lend his support to Egypt's roughly 250,000 Catholics and insist on the protection of minority rights, including those of its nearly 10 million Coptic Christians, in a meeting Friday with Mr. Sisi, according to Samir Khalil Samir, an Egyptian-born Jesuit priest who has seen the pope's prepared remarks.

He will also meet with Sheikh Ahmed al-Tayeb, the grand imam of Al Azhar mosque, which is affiliated with a university that is a revered center of learning in Sunni Islam, and speak at a peace conference organized by the mosque. The pope finishes the day by meeting his Coptic Christian counterpart, Pope Tawadros II, who escaped one of the bombings on Palm Sunday.

"It's an encounter of consolation, promotion and communion with the small Catholic community," said Cardinal Leonardo Sandri, the prefect for the Congregation for Eastern Churches, who is to join Francis on the trip. "But it's of great importance from an ecumenical point of view. And, of course, it is very important for dialogue with Islam, for the meeting with the sheikh of Al Ahzar."

Like Pope John Paul II, who in 2000 became the first modern pope to visit Egypt, Francis is a politically attuned global player. It is perhaps no accident that he drew attention to his remarks about Christian martyrs last weekend by comparing the Greek refugee camp — where he said he met the Muslim husband of the slain Christian woman — to a "concentration camp."

His predecessor, Pope Benedict XVI, was less adroit. He stumbled into a public relations disaster in 2006 at the University of Regensburg in Germany when he quoted a 14th century Byzantine emperor suggesting fanaticism was inherent to Islam. That set the tone for a rocky relationship with Islam.

But Pope Francis, who received Sheikh Tayeb last year at the Vatican in a visit that restored relations, has a greater bank of good will because of his outreach to the Muslim world.

Francis has washed the feet of Muslims during the Holy Thursday Mass, and in 2016 he washed the feet of Muslim, Hindu, Catholic and Coptic Christian migrants — a ritual that demonstrates humility and the notion that even the pope must serve his fellow man. During a trip last year to the Greek island of Lesbos, where he met the Muslim man who told him about the slaying of his Christian wife, he took 12 Muslim refugees back to Rome on the papal plane.

But he has also repeatedly, and clearly, drawn attention to the killings of Christians in Muslim countries like Egypt.

In 2013, during his first Easter season as pope, he asked the faithful to pray “especially for Christians who suffer persecution.” In 2014, he wrote a letter to all persecuted Christians in the Middle East, demanding “that all religious leaders clearly speak out to condemn these crimes” and he denounced “invoking religion in order to justify” the crimes.

He spoke in support of “Egyptian martyrs” in 2015 whose “throats were cut as they pronounced Jesus’ name.” And last year, he took the opportunity of the feast of St. Stephen, Christianity’s first martyr, to note that “the number of martyrs today is greater than in the early centuries.”

Some corners of the pope’s own church, though, think he has not gone far enough. They have balked at the logo for the trip to Egypt, which shows a cross and a crescent moon together. “Mr. Coexist,” one conservative Catholic blog sniped.

His remarks to reporters after the killing of a Catholic priest by jihadists in France last year vexed many conservatives in the church. “I don’t think it is right to equate Islam with violence,” he told reporters. “If I have to talk about Islamic violence, I have to talk about Christian violence. Every day in the newspapers I see violence in Italy, someone kills his girlfriend, another kills his mother-in-law, and these are baptized Catholics.”

Francis has studiously maintained that aversion to criticism, even in private.

Last June, Father Samir, the Egyptian priest and a leading Catholic scholar of Islam, met with the pope to talk about Islam at the pope’s apartment in Vatican City. Before the meeting, Father Samir sent the pope articles he had written noting that the Quran contained both peaceful and violent passages.

When Father Samir broached the topic, he said the pope countered that his experiences with an imam in Argentina left him with the impression that Islam was peaceful and that he viewed his mission as re-establishing good relations with Muslims.

Father Samir said he gently countered that he himself could not be blind to the negative aspects of Islam, that both needed to be considered, but that the pope seemed to have little interest in the subject. "So he simply passed to other things," Father Samir said in an interview, adding that "his knowledge of Islam is limited to the nice discussions he had with the imam."

Despite his critique, Father Samir said he had seen an advance copy of the pope's address to Mr. Sisi, which he considered strong and diplomatic for its emphasis on protecting the rights of all minorities.

That is a message top Vatican officials have emphasized.

"It is necessary to have a very strong protection of Christians; they are citizens with religious rights," Cardinal Sandri said. "Especially from a point of view of religious freedom, we must consider all citizens the same."

The Vatican released a video message on Tuesday of the pope greeting the Egyptian people ahead of his trip, in what Francis called a world "torn by blind violence, which has also afflicted the heart of your dear land."

"I hope that this visit will be an embrace of consolation and of encouragement to all Christians in the Middle East," he said, adding that he carried a message of reconciliation, "particularly in the Islamic world."

Pope Defends His Myanmar Diplomacy: 'I Did Not Negotiate With the Truth'

BY JASON HOROWITZ | DEC. 2, 2017

ABOARD THE PAPAL PLANE — After breaking his silence on the plight of Myanmar's persecuted Muslim minority in a moving encounter on Friday with refugees in Bangladesh, Pope Francis wanted to keep talking about the Rohingya, and saying their name, on the way back to Rome on Saturday.

"I would prefer you first ask questions about the visit," the pope said in a news conference aboard his plane.

He was responding to a reporter who had asked about a development in the church's teaching on nuclear weapons, from accepting nuclear deterrence to insisting on total disarmament. The reporter wanted to know whether the insults between President Trump and the North Korean leader Kim Jong-un had contributed to that change.

"What has changed? The irrationality has changed," the pope answered.

The pontiff then let it be known that when it came to questions, "it would please me to have some more on the trip."

After days of critical coverage about his not uttering the word "Rohingya" while in Myanmar, the politically savvy pope seemed eager to discuss what he considered the success of a trip that even his supporters had warned was a stumble into a political minefield.

"I am very, very satisfied with the meetings," he said.

In his nearly hourlong remarks, the pope sought to explain his approach to effective diplomacy ("one half step back, one step forward") and strategic communications ("the most important thing is that the message gets across") and even offered his geopolitical analysis, explaining that someone had told him that the area of Myanmar where the Rohingya lived was "rich in precious stones" and that outside interests perhaps wanted it emptied for mining. "But I don't know if it's true," he said.

He called the meeting with the Rohingya in Dhaka, Bangladesh, a "condition of the trip," and opened up about the emotions he experienced visiting with 16 survivors of the persecution, to whom he vowed: "We won't close our hearts or look away. The presence of God today is also called Rohingya."

Aboard the plane, the pope flashed a defensive streak about his avoidance of using the politically contentious word during his days in Myanmar.

"If I had said that word in the official speeches, it would have been a door slammed in the face," he said, using a metaphor he turned to several times, and which he said evoked for him the image of how an angry teenager vents frustration.

"It's true I didn't have the pleasure of slamming the door in their face publicly with a denunciation," the pope said. "But I had the satisfaction of dialogue, and letting the other side dialogue, and in this way the message arrived."

He argued that his caution granted him access to private meetings, where he could be more frank.

Of his meeting with Senior Gen. Min Aung Hlaing, who has led a campaign of mass murder, rape and arson against the Rohingya, the pope said that "I did not negotiate with the truth" during the conversation and that he made the general understand that the horrors of the past were no longer viable.

The general had demanded to meet with Pope Francis before the pontiff saw Myanmar's de facto leader, Daw Aung San Suu Kyi, the Nobel Peace Prize laureate whose reputation has suffered for her failure to forcefully condemn the killings. (The pope suggested she be cut some slack, saying, "In Myanmar, it's difficult to evaluate a criticism without asking, 'Is it possible to have done this?' ")

When a reporter asked the pope if he worried he had been used as a political pawn by the general to show the country who was boss, the pope said, "The intention of that I do not know, but I was interested in dialogue." Pressed if he had used the word "Rohingya" in the private meeting, he responded that once he made sure the general understood his message, "I dared say everything I wanted to say."

All of that diplomatic work, the pope suggested, was done to encourage Myanmar, a country "at the tipping point," to push ahead toward democracy. And he likewise suggested that his silence on the Rohingya paid off with the trip's culminating meeting with the refugees in Dhaka on Friday.

He pointed out that TG1, an Italian news program, dedicated a long segment to the meeting. "You saw today the front pages of the papers. All of them have received the message. And I have not heard any criticism. Maybe there is, but I haven't heard it."

The old Francis charm, he seemed to be saying, was back in action.

ADAM DEAN FOR THE NEW YORK TIMES

A Rohingya refugee at the Kutupalong camp in Cox's Bazar, Bangladesh, November 2017. More than 600,000 Rohingya have fled to neighboring Bangladesh.

At different points of the trip, humanitarian activists had wondered where his special touch had gone. They expressed disappointment that Pope Francis, admired for speaking out for the downtrodden, had gone quiet for fear of endangering his own flock in Myanmar. Some analysts questioned how it affected his moral authority. Locals doubted his influence.

Last Monday, when the pope arrived in Yangon, Myanmar, and met with General Min Aung Hlaing, a woman, Hla Yin Win, 31, was walking around the city's revered pagoda complex with her husband and baby daughter. She stopped in front of a wood shrine with gold-painted pillars dedicated by Buddhist faithful from the Rakhine State, where the Rohingya have been persecuted.

Ms. Win said that she liked the general "because the military power is important for our country," that she appreciated the soldiers "doing their duty" and that she considered the Rohingya, who had been in the country for generations, "illegal immigrants who don't speak Burmese and are bad for our country."

Asked if she thought the pope could make a difference in the crisis, she shook her head.

"He doesn't matter," she said.

On the plane the pope reminded why he did matter. He relived in detail the meeting with Rohingya refugees at a packed interreligious meeting in the garden of the Dhaka archbishop's residence.

He explained that at the end of the event, the 16 men, women and children came up to the stage, but that organizers "immediately wanted to kick them off the scene. That's when I got angry. I yelled a bit."

He met with them individually and added that he could not let them leave without saying a word.

"In that moment, I began to feel things inside. I was crying but I tried to hide it. They were crying too," he said. "So I asked for the microphone," and that is when the pope finally said, "Rohingya."

Why the Pope Is Genuflecting to China

OPINION | BY YI-ZHENG LIAN | FEB. 8, 2018

ON FEB. 1, the same day that new repressive regulations of religion went into force in China, the Vatican took a deep bow before Beijing. After long resisting, it finally agreed to recognize several hack bishops designated by the Chinese Communist Party (C.C.P.), even sidelining two of its own long-serving appointees for the occasion.

Cardinal Joseph Zen Ze-kiun, the outspoken, blogging, 86-year-old retired archbishop of Hong Kong, had recently flown to Vatican City to personally plead the case of the two bishops to the pope himself. How nettlesome. He was shoved off, and has since been called an "obstacle" to a deal between the Vatican and Beijing.

The reasons the Holy See is caving to the (atheist) Communist government are not entirely transparent, but it appears to be hoping for a historic thaw. Diplomatic ties were severed in 1951, not long after the Communists came to power in China, and relations have since been testy at best.

Catholics in China are thought to number between 9 million and 12 million today, with about half of them adhering to underground congregations loyal to the pope in Rome and refusing to recognize a state-sanctioned version of the Church called the Chinese Catholic Patriotic Association or, more informally, the "patriotic church."

One major conflict between the two governments has been the method for appointing bishops: Traditionally a prerogative of the papacy, Beijing has steadily tried to usurp it in China. The deal that the Vatican currently seems to be seeking would likely formalize some joint vetting procedure.

The Vatican justifies its conciliatory stance toward Beijing as an attempt to overcome the schism that has divided the Catholic community in China for nearly seven decades — as "a balm of mercy," it has said, for the pain caused by the barriers that have prevented Chinese Catholics "from living in communion with each other and with the Pope."

Rapprochement could also give the pope, nominally at least, ultimate authority over all the Catholics in China — a standing, however symbolic, that may well matter to a Vatican that is losing ground to other Christian denominations among Chinese converts.

The total population of Christians in China has grown considerably, from about 4 million in 1949 to perhaps as many as 100 million today. In relative terms, however, Catholics are falling behind. By some estimates, whereas Catholics in China outnumbered Protestants by 3 to 1 in 1949, today Protestants outnumber Catholics by 5 to 1.

A major explanation for the increasing differential is that the Roman Catholic Church wields not only religious and moral authority, but also political and diplomatic power.

The Catholic Church has a relatively unified command structure, a well-defined ideology and a disciplined organizational backbone. It has global reach and mass appeal, commands great loyalty and has long demonstrated the ability to survive and expand, all on the merits of peaceful soft power. In each of these ways, it rivals, perhaps even bests, the C.C.P.

And so, naturally, the C.C.P. sees Chinese Catholics' allegiance to the pope as a direct challenge to their allegiance to the party. Vatican City is also, still, among the 20 states, all small, that recognize Taiwan diplomatically.

Many Protestant churches, although deemed suspect as well, are on better terms with the C.C.P. After a visit to Beijing in 1983, the archbishop of Canterbury gushed about liberalization in China and reportedly praised the emergence of "a church with Chinese characteristics."

Like his predecessor, the current Anglican archbishop overseeing Hong Kong and Macau is a member of the Chinese People's Political Consultative Conference, a body including luminaries that supposedly advises the C.C.P. but often promotes the party's interests informally or clandestinely. Both men have tended to support Beijing's restrictive reading of democratic freedoms in Hong Kong and opposed the pro-democracy Umbrella Movement of 2014.

Representatives of other faiths have gone further. A vice president of the Buddhist Association of China called President Xi Jinping's speech to the Chinese Communist Party's 19th Congress last fall, "the Buddhist sutra of the current age." Buddhists in China — who are variously said to number between more than 100 million to more than 240 million — have been treated with a relatively light hand by the party, at least if they are not of the Tibetan kind.

Yet even if brown-nosing seems to pay off, the Vatican's appeasement of the Chinese government would have great downsides, for itself and for the rest of the world.

By recognizing China's so-called patriotic church, the Vatican could harm the wholesomeness of Catholic teachings in the country. Sermons given in government-sanctioned churches already have been known to exclude passages of the Bible deemed politically subversive (like the story of Daniel) or to include Communist Party propaganda.

Millions of faithful Catholics in China might also soon feel abandoned, perhaps even betrayed, after having suffered decades of oppression. Worse, the government, emboldened by the deal, could well come down even harder on them. In fact, the religious regulations that recently came into effect include much stiffer fines on underground churches and penalties for public-school teachers who give Sunday-school lessons on their own time.

And then, rapprochement might augur the Vatican's readiness to eventually stop recognizing Taipei and instead recognize Beijing as truly representing China. Such a shift would alter the delicate balance of power across the Taiwan Strait, as well as harm Taiwan's vibrant democracy. It would also confer legitimacy — and with the pope's imprimatur! — on authoritarian regimes throughout the world that crack down on churches and sects.

The Catholic Church already has a checkered record dealing with fascist or totalitarian states. Pope Pius XII was criticized for betraying the Jews of Europe during World War II: Hewing to what he described as a position of neutrality between the Nazis and the Allies, he never denounced Hitler's Final Solution. After Soviet forces violently repressed the Hungarian uprising in 1956, the Vatican sidelined the outspoken anticommunist Archbishop József Mindszenty in favor of a deal with the new puppet regime.

The Vatican's eagerness to play catch-up in China today may do it no favors either.

Beijing doesn't have much of a reputation for honoring commitments. Just look at its application of the "one country, two systems" arrangement it promised Hong Kong, which was supposed to guarantee the city a large degree of autonomy until 2047.

Even under the deal the Vatican seems to want, the Chinese government could eventually come to control the Catholic Church in China — by, say, simply delaying nominating anyone for bishop or repeatedly rejecting candidates presented by the Vatican until all the bishops previously selected by the pope have retired or died out. Bishops ordain priests and so without bishops, in time there could be no priests, or very few, and Catholicism in China would have died a silent death.

Four decades ago, when a destitute China was emerging from deep Maoism, Western companies got tipsy at the mere notion of selling deodorant to two billion Chinese armpits. Now that average Chinese have much more disposable income, major international corporations are willing to hand over proprietary technology, stoically endure violent xenophobic outbursts and take on members of the Chinese Communist Party as senior managers rather than risk losing out on the business prospects.

No one, it seems, can resist the lure of the great market of China, for deodorants, cars — or congregants. Not even the Vatican.

YI-ZHENG LIAN, a commentator on Hong Kong and Asian affairs, is a professor of economics at Yamanashi Gakuin University, in Kofu, Japan.

A Pope Given to Apologies Has Nothing for Indigenous Canada

BY IAN AUSTEN AND JASON HOROWITZ | APRIL 23, 2018

OTTAWA — The past three popes have invested deeply in the forgiveness-begging business, offering official apologies for the church's sins against Jews during World War II and Indigenous people in Bolivia, among others.

But Canada's Roman Catholic bishops said late last month that Pope Francis would not apologize in the foreseeable future for the boarding schools where, for more than a century and a half, more than 150,000 Indigenous children were forced to attend in an effort to obliterate their cultures and languages.

About 70 percent of children went to schools operated by the church.

Now, the Canadian House of Commons is poised to consider a motion to ask those bishops to return to Rome to seek a papal apology, fulfilling a specific recommendation for healing the rift between Canada and its Indigenous people by a national Truth and Reconciliation Commission that documented the abuses at the schools.

"This wasn't the work of a few bad apples," said Charlie Angus, a practicing Catholic and New Democratic Party member of Parliament who introduced the motion, which is supported by the government and likely to pass. "The church's role was enormous."

"I've seen very little pushback to my motion from Catholics," Mr. Angus added. "People just don't understand how after all the information that's come out why the church isn't moving on this."

Thousands died in the schools, and many were victims of physical and sexual abuse. Some priests and nuns at the Catholic schools were involved in the most depraved abuses, including at an Ontario school where students were shocked on a homemade electric chair.

Since the release of the letter from the Canadian Conference of Catholic Bishops saying the pope would not apologize now, Canada's bishops have offered little clarity about why. Several Catholic lay people in Canada, including some who have worked within the church, say they believe the pontiff is following the advice of the Canadian bishops, who generally oppose the idea.

Some bishops in western Canada and the north — where most of the schools were — do support an apology. When the letter was released, Bishop Mark Hagemoen in Saskatoon, Saskatchewan, noted the disappointment of the Indigenous community in a statement, adding, "I too regret that Pope Francis is not coming at this time." The presumption is that an apology would be made during a visit.

Other bishops, in east Canada, say they believe that the church has already apologized and that in any event the pope's actions shouldn't be dictated by a government commission. They also are concerned about the cost of any papal visit because local dioceses would bear the expenses.

In recent years, papal infallibility, a concept officially codified by Pius IX nearly 150 years ago, seems to have been supplanted by papal apology.

Seven years before the death of John Paul II, in 2005, an Italian journalist, Luigi Accattoli, counted the pope as making at least 94 apologies. And that was before some of his big ones, like his "Day of Pardon" apology for the church's sins against Jews, heretics, Gypsies, native peoples and women.

Pope Benedict XVI continued the trend, though the theologian argued that apologies were for the actions of individual Christians. His milestone apology went to clerical sexual abuse victims in Ireland.

Francis also has said sorry time and again — but never more forcefully and poignantly than he did this month in a letter to Chilean bishops that came after his own missteps on the sexual abuse issue that threatened to stain his papacy.

He first dismissed as "slander" accusations that a Chilean bishop had covered up abuse. The resulting outrage, the harshest he had faced in his papacy, led him to send his top investigator to Chile. The result was a remarkable apology.

"I recognize and I want you to communicate this accurately, that I have made serious errors of judgment and perception of the situation, especially due to lack of truthful and balanced information," Francis wrote.

So now would seem a particularly good time to ask for an apology. And if Canada's bishops supported it, it is hard to see that the pope would refuse because a hallmark of the Francis papacy is to decentralize authority to the bishops conferences around the world.

Joe Gunn, who spent a decade at the bishops' conference in Canada helping to develop policies related to Indigenous people, said bishops in Ontario and Quebec whose diocese had little or no direct involvement in the notorious schools, likely blocked efforts to recommend a visit and an apology.

Financial concerns most likely factored in, if a papal visit were part of the apology, Mr. Gunn and others suggested. A 2002 visit to Canada by Pope John Paul II left the Canadian bishops' conference 36 million Canadian dollars in debt. The shortfall was covered by the country's dioceses, financially straining some.

But Mr. Gunn, who is now the executive director of Citizens for Public Justice, a faith-based public policy group, said the bishops' stance more likely reflected a fractured church in Canada, as well as a general lack of a national strategy on reconciliation.

"Each diocese and institute is corporately and legally responsible for its own actions," the bishops wrote in a recent statement. "The Catholic Church as a whole in Canada was not associated with the residential schools, nor was the Canadian Conference of Catholic Bishops."

That assertion, though, has been widely rejected.

"It's convenient when you have an issue like this to not have the responsibility shared nationally," Mr. Gunn said. "Contrast that with when the bishops speak about other issues like abortion. They don't use the same kind of language."

As the public backlash in Canada has grown over the lack of an apology, the bishops have also adopted the position that there have, in fact, already been papal apologies for residential schools.

In particular, they cite a private meeting in 2009 between Pope Benedict and Indigenous leaders, including Phil Fontaine, then the leader of the Assembly of First Nations, the country's largest aboriginal group. At that time, the pope expressed his "sorrow" about the schools.

Few people other than the bishops, however, equate the pope's words at that meeting with an apology — including Mr. Fontaine.

"It was right for the moment," Mr. Fontaine said this past week about Pope Benedict's expression of sorrow. "But there's a lot we didn't know about in 2009: We didn't know the number of deaths, the numbers of those abused. So much has been exposed through the Truth and Reconciliation Commission, it's really so different now."

Father Tom Rosica, the chief executive of Salt and Light Media, a Catholic television service based in Toronto, is among those in the church bristling at the idea of Canada's Parliament, or any government, issuing demands of the pope.

"Governments never dictate to the pope what the pope should say and when he should say it," said Father Rosica, who has worked in the Vatican's media office.

But Mr. Angus, the lawmaker who introduced the motion, which is likely to be debated late this week, said that because the church ran the schools on behalf of the government using government money, the measure does not inappropriately cross any lines between politics and religion.

While Canada has no constitutional separation between church and state, it is unusual for Parliament in modern times to make a request of any church.

During a recent news conference, Archbishop Richard Gagnon of Winnipeg, Manitoba, endorsed the pope's decision not to offer an apology now.

But Archbishop Gagnon and Bishop Lionel Gendron, the president of the bishops' conference, repeatedly avoided answering direct questions about advice they had given the pope, and they did not offer much guidance about when they thought a visit and apology might be appropriate.

"If you place Pope Francis among Indigenous people and he hears these horrible stories, what do you think he's going to say?" Archbishop Gagnon told reporters.

IAN AUSTEN reported from Ottawa, and **JASON HOROWITZ** from Rome.

The Pope vs. the Populists

OPINION | BY IVAN KRASTEV | MAY 2, 2018

DEBATING THE FATE of Poland during the waning days of World War II, Winston Churchill is reported to have cautioned Joseph Stalin that he should take into account the views of the Vatican. The Soviet leader interrupted Churchill: "How many divisions does the pope of Rome have?" Three decades later, Churchill's admonition seemed prescient: The election of the Polish Cardinal Karol Wojtyla as Pope John Paul II in 1978 was a first step leading to the dismantling of Soviet Communism.

Amid today's heated rhetoric on Europe's refugee crisis, Central Europe's populist leaders seem to paraphrase Stalin: "How many elections has the pope won?" It is a serious question. The day before Pope Francis issued an apostolic exhortation with the message that caring for migrants should be as important to Catholics as their opposition to abortion, Prime Minister Viktor Orban of Hungary, a self-styled defender of Christianity, won a landslide electoral victory with the message that welcoming migrants is worse than abortion.

Why are citizens in post-Communist countries with Catholic majorities unmoved by the message of Pope Francis? Why has the rise of right-wing parties like Law and Justice in Poland and Fidesz in Hungary, which claim a strong affiliation with Catholic identity and attract the support of many believers, resulted in open conflict with the Vatican? Does the rise of populism in Central Europe signal the return of religion or further secularization of society?

Last year, Pew Research published a report on the role of religion in post-Communist countries that suggests some possible answers. The report makes clear that the resurgence of religion since the end of Communism has played out differently in the predominantly Orthodox countries of Eastern Europe than among the Catholic states of Central Europe. In the Orthodox countries like Russia, Bulgaria and Romania, there has been an upsurge of religious identity, but levels of religious practice are comparatively low. People define themselves as Orthodox Christians though they rarely go to church or read the Bible. For them, Orthodox identity is bound up with national identity, feelings of pride and cultural superiority. Sociologists call it "belonging without believing."

In historically Catholic countries like Poland, Hungary, Lithuania and the Czech Republic, the share of adults who identify as Catholic has declined since the end of Communism. Levels of church attendance and other measures of religious observance are generally higher than in their Orthodox neighbors, but in Catholic-majority countries there is also a growing tendency to view the church as a national institution rather than a spiritual one.

In this context, tensions between the Vatican and Catholic communities in Central Europe should not come as a surprise. They are an expression of the new role of Europe in the Catholic world. We are accustomed to viewing Catholicism as a European religion, but that hasn't been the case in quite some time. Although 70 percent of Orthodox Christians live on the old continent, most Catholics today reside outside Europe — in Latin America and, increasingly, Asia and Africa.

As the New York Times columnist Ross Douthat has argued, while much of the world is in love with Pope Francis, many believers and clergymen mistrust him and fear that his papacy might be a disaster. Rejection of the non-European pope is particularly strong in Central Europe. Many Catholics in Poland and Hungary view Pope Francis the way die-hard Communists and party apparatchiks viewed the Soviet leader Mikhail Gorbachev during the height of "Gorbymania" in the late 1980s — a dangerous revisionist corrupted by media attention who threatens the integrity and power of their faith. In Poland, when people talk about the pope, they usually mean John Paul II.

But the populist right and the Catholic Church in Central Europe are hardly a match made in heaven. For the populists, Christianity is not so much a relationship between man and God as a relation between one community and another. Populism's ascent can be more effectively explained by the public's fears about the spread of Islam rather than by any affinity with the religious teachings of Catholicism.

A good Christian, not unlike a populist voter, is expected to live in constant fear. But while Christian believers should fear that they will do something wrong, populist voters constantly fear that others will do something wrong to them. In other words, the fear preached by the church is just the opposite of the politics of fear preached by the populists.

Sociologists have demonstrated that practicing Catholics in Poland and Hungary are more likely than others to vote for right-wing populist parties. At the same time, the governments in Hungary and Poland do not miss an opportunity to show their commitment to the church, whether through rhetoric or with policies like strict abortion bans. The bishops of Central Europe have enjoyed these overtures. But they may want to rethink this policy. The romance between the church and the populist right could easily turn into a spiritual crisis.

The dilemma that the Catholic Church faces in Central Europe is whether it is ready to allow populist leaders to speak not only in the name of the people but also in the name of God. Could an anti-populist backlash also turn against the church? Urban liberals in places like Poland, while sympathizing with Pope Francis' message on issues such as climate change or the moral failings of contemporary society, increasingly see the Catholic Church as an enemy, while conservative believers are turning to populist politicians as their spiritual leaders. In the end, the rise of populism could achieve what Communists never managed to do: divorce church and society in Central Europe.

IVAN KRASTEV is a contributing opinion writer, the chairman of the Center for Liberal Strategies, a permanent fellow at the Institute for Human Sciences in Vienna and the author, most recently, of "After Europe."

As Ireland Joins Europe's Sprint From Catholic Fold, Francis Looks South

BY JASON HOROWITZ | MAY 27, 2018

VATICAN CITY — When nearly one-third of Ireland's Catholic population came to see Pope John Paul II celebrate a papal Mass in Dublin in 1979, divorce, homosexual acts and abortion were all illegal in the country. Ireland, like much of Europe, toed the line on Roman Catholic Church teaching.

In August, Pope Francis will return to Ireland for a World Meeting of Families event attended by the church's most committed anti-abortion activists. But they will find themselves, after Saturday's historic repeal of an abortion ban in a landslide vote, in a country that is clearly part of Europe's secular sprint out of the Roman Catholic fold.

Across Western Europe, the church's once mighty footprint has faded, in no small measure because of self-inflicted clerical sex abuse scandals and an inability to keep up with and reach contemporary Catholics. Church attendance has plummeted, parishes are merging, and new priests and nuns are in short supply. Gay marriage is on the rise, and abortion is widely legal.

And yet, Francis is not sounding the alarm or calling the faithful to the ramparts. He seems resigned to accept that a devout and Catholic Europe has largely slipped into the church's past.

Instead, he has shifted his focus on the faith's future to the global South from which he came. At the heart of Francis' vision is a closeness of priests to the poor and desolate whom he believes the church should most serve.

This turn has drawn criticism from conservative Catholics like those in the Continent's most faithful country, Poland, who have allied with a nationalist government to keep out migrants.

But the Argentine pontiff clearly believes that emphasizing a poor church ministering to the world's outcasts is a more authentic, appealing — and ultimately evangelizing — global message than a defense of orthodoxy and Europe's Christian roots.

The challenge for Francis is to keep the present decline of the church in Europe from becoming a preview of its future in South America and Africa.

Inoculating the Southern Hemisphere from the growing scourge of sex abuse scandals, spreading secularism and out-of-touch clergy that devastated Catholicism in Europe is no easy task and will require much of the pope's attention.

This may explain why Francis, while silent about Ireland before the vote, has been remarkably focused this month on a sex abuse scandal in Chile, threatening the church's credibility there.

"The sex abuse scandal and the negligence of bishops in Chile has done enormous damage," said Juan-Carlos Cruz, a sex abuse survivor who recently met with the pope. He said he hoped the Vatican would hold bishops accountable and give that strategy a chance to succeed in Chile. The failure to address the crisis, he said, had caused a "rapid climb of secularism in countries that were the hope of expansion for the church."

The church's looming problems outside Europe's borders don't stop with sexual abuse.

In Latin America and Africa, where the future of the church seems most promising, there are also signs it is losing ground in a bustling religious marketplace.

In Brazil, which has the world's largest Catholic population, evangelicals preaching prosperity gospels are giving stiff competition to Catholicism, which is projected to become a minority faith in 2030. Francis made Brazil his first trip overseas after his election.

Whereas Francis sees a focus on the poor as the church's greatest hope, his predecessor, Benedict XVI, a German, saw secularism as the greatest threat to the church's future. His pre-election homily against the "dictatorship of relativism" helped get him the job, and his papacy was considered by many as a last-ditch effort to save Europe and its Christian roots. But the European erosion continued unchecked, and Benedict called it quits in 2013.

To find his successor, cardinals searched "the ends of the Earth," as Francis said, and chose the first non-European cardinal in nearly 1,300 years. Vatican analysts said the church had recognized that its future lay elsewhere.

Five years into his papacy, Francis' radical reprioritization on the world's poor has imbued much of the Vatican. In Sunday's L'Osservatore Romano, the official newspaper of the Vatican, news about the referendum in Ireland sank below headlines about Libyan human smugglers opening fire on fleeing migrants, and about the pope's advocacy for a more ethical financial system.

In wealthy Europe, though, the church's woes show few signs of abating.

Last week, in an address to the Italian Bishops Conference, Francis suggested that it was time to cluster together some of the hundreds of Italian parishes around the country. He asked the Italians to be creative in thinking about how to revive the church.

In Italy, many Catholic parishes are now operated by clergy born outside the country.

In mostly Catholic Luxembourg, the government, led by a gay prime minister, abolished religious teaching in state schools in September. In 2012, the Archdiocese of Vienna consolidated its 660 parishes into 150.

Only one-in-five Catholics attend Mass in Spain now. In France, it's one in 10. In the Netherlands, Mass attendance among Catholics is down to about 5 percent. In Germany, financial contributions to the church have thinned.

In Ireland, this week's vote was only the latest leap away from a church that long dominated the country's culture. Ireland had already voted to legalize gay marriage.

"The Catholic Church's hold on the people has diminished," said Mary McAuliffe, a lecturer in gender studies at University College

Dublin. "There is no denying that, and particularly largely through self-inflicted wounds."

The church largely kept out of the referendum campaign, in part because anti-abortion activists believed the involvement of an institution so tarnished by scandals would only help the repeal effort.

Benedict recognized the danger of the sex abuse scandals to the church in Ireland, and in 2010 sent an extraordinary pastoral letter to Catholics there, saying "I can only share in the dismay and the sense of betrayal that so many of you have experienced."

The letter also argued that the church operated as a force for good in Irish society, through schools, hospitals and charities, and that the country's Catholics "helped to consolidate the spiritual identity of Europe." But he also noted that the abuse scandals occurred amid "secularization of Irish society" with the result a "weakening of faith and the loss of respect for the Church."

The Irish church never really recovered. But there are pockets of the devout in Europe — it's just that they often disagree with the current pope's priorities.

By most measures, Poland is the most faithful Catholic country in Europe. About 40 percent of Catholics attend Sunday Mass, nearly everyone is baptized, and it actually exports its priests to other European countries. The strong faith is in part because of Saint John Paul II, an enormously charismatic pope who became central to Polish identity and its sense of liberation from Communism.

But there is also a more contemporary convergence between the traditional Christian values that John Paul promoted and the nationalism of President Andrzej Duda's governing Law and Justice Party, which opposes Francis' calls to accept migrants and to combat global climate change.

Anger toward Francis sometimes rises to the surface.

Monsignor Edward Staniek, a prominent Polish priest who is intent on protecting traditional Catholic values from secularization, said earlier this year that he prayed Francis would agree with his thinking on the problem or have "a quick passage to the house of the Father."

In Hungary, many church officials have allied with the anti-immigrant prime minister, Viktor Orban, who comes from a Protestant background and was once ambivalent about religion but who now says, "European identity is rooted in Christianity."

He considers his fence against migrants a defense of Western civilization, and Bishop Laszlo Kiss-Rigo, the church's top official in southern Hungary, apparently agrees, having said that the pope doesn't understand the situation and that Hungary is under invasion.

Populists in Italy have said Francis is essentially abandoning the fight for Europe's Christian identity. Matteo Salvini, the leader of the anti-immigrants League party, has talked about how Pope Benedict understood the needs of European nations to keep their religious and cultural identity in the face of Muslim migration.

If the landslide vote in Ireland bothered Francis, he didn't show it on Sunday afternoon. He smiled broadly as he blessed tens of thousands of people in St. Peter's Square and urged them to pray for Africa.

Kilvia Passos, 47, cheered the pope as she held a flag of her native Brazil, the country with the world's largest Catholic population. She said despite the growing competition of evangelicals there, the country still felt deeply Catholic.

But so, until a few decades ago, did Ireland and the rest of Europe.

"We're worried about what's happening here," she said.

MEGAN SPECIA contributed reporting from New York.

CHAPTER 5

The Challenge of Reforming a Church in Crisis

The Vatican is notorious for the complexity of its politics, divided between progressive and traditionalist factions made more complex by the longevity of the church's many institutions. Though elected as a reformer, Francis' progressive moves have entangled him in church politics, inspiring a faction of conservative dissenters. The revelation of child sexual abuse by priests, first recognized in the early 2000s, has inflamed these tensions into a full-blown crisis. Francis' struggles to take an authoritative position on this crisis have left the future of his papacy in doubt.

Pope Is Quoted Referring to a Vatican 'Gay Lobby'

BY RACHEL DONADIO | JUNE 12, 2013

ROME — For years, perhaps even centuries, it has been an open secret in Rome: That some prelates in the Vatican hierarchy are gay. But the whispers were amplified this week when Pope Francis himself, in a private audience, appears to have acknowledged what he called a "gay lobby" operating inside the Vatican, vying for power and influence.

The remarks — which the Vatican spokesman did not deny and the participants at the private audience confirmed — appeared to be part of an effort by the pope to take on the entrenched interests in the Vatican that many believe were a factor in why the previous pope, Benedict XVI, resigned unexpectedly. They appear to underscore numerous reports in the prelude to the election of the pope, that corruption, blackmail and violation of one of the highest codes of Catholic conduct were part of the intrigue that scandalized the Vatican in recent years.

Francis, who portrays himself as a simple pope of the people, has made it clear that one of his highest priorities is to put the Vatican's house in order. He has appointed a group of eight cardinals to advise him on how to overhaul the Vatican, and the head of the Vatican Bank has recently given a series of interviews to journalists — an openness unheard of under his predecessors.

"It's pretty incredible that the pope said these things," said Sandro Magister, a Vatican expert at the Italian weekly L'Espresso. "I don't think there's any doubt on the foundation of the phrases attributed to him. Otherwise they would have denied it."

The pope made the remarks at the Vatican on June 6, while speaking to a meeting of the Latin American and Caribbean Confederation of Religious, the regional organization for priests and nuns of religious orders.

"In the Curia, there are also holy people, really, there are holy people. But there also is a stream of corruption, there is that as well, it is true," he said in Spanish, according to a loose summary of the meeting posted on a Chilean Web site, Reflection and Liberation, and later translated into English by the blog Rorate Caeli.

"The 'gay lobby' is mentioned, and it is true, it is there ... We need to see what we can do," Francis continued, in the document, produced here verbatim.

On Tuesday, the Vatican spokesman, the Rev. Federico Lombardi, did not deny the reports of Francis' remarks, saying only that he had no comment on a private meeting — a marked shift from past months, in which the Vatican vehemently called such reports "unverified, unverifiable or completely false."

Also on Tuesday, the Latin American group, known by its Spanish acronym CLAR, confirmed the remarks and issued an apology, saying it was distressed that its summary had been published.

Long the subject of speculation in Vatican circles, the term gay lobby had emerged most recently in juicy, unsourced reports in the Italian daily newspaper La Repubblica and a news weekly, Panorama, before the March conclave in which Francis, the former Cardinal Jorge Mario Bergoglio of Buenos Aires, was elected.

Before his retirement on Feb. 28, the reports said, Benedict had been worn down by corruption scandals — including what they said was a network of gay priests inside the Vatican who used blackmail to gain influence and trade in state secrets.

A secret dossier compiled by three cardinals Benedict had asked to investigate a leaks scandal at the Vatican last year had revealed the network, which also included lay people who were aware of gay clerics inside the Vatican and who were in a position to blackmail them, the reports said.

Veteran watchers of the Roman Curia were unfazed by Francis' remarks. One Vatican official, speaking on the traditional condition of anonymity, said he was not surprised that Francis had spoken of a gay lobby, but noted that the summary lacked "context and tone."

"If you have an institution as big as the Vatican, there are some who will be homosexual, some maybe actively so," the official said. "But whether there's collusion or internal cooperation, I've certainly not been aware of it."

Others said that the remarks were in line with the new pope's emphasis on openness.

"A lobby of those who blackmail each other proliferates if you don't talk about it, if there's no air," said Alberto Melloni, a Vatican historian and director of the John XXIII Foundation for Religious Studies in Bologna, a liberal Catholic research institute. "He's right to talk about it, it breaks the mechanism in which omertà favors the use of blackmail. If no one talks about it, it's a powerful weapon. In that way, he's cut the issue down to size and conveys the sense that reforming the Curia is easy."

"This is a question of blackmail and blackmailability, not homosexuality," he added.

Two of the biggest internal threats to Benedict's papacy, including a scandal of leaked documents, were driven by factions within the Vatican who used leaked information to vie for power. Those scandals contributed to Benedict's decision to retire.

Writing in La Repubblica on Tuesday, the Vatican expert Paolo Rodari said that Francis had also mentioned the gay lobby in a meeting last month with bishops from Sicily.

In the summary of Francis' remarks to the Latin American group, the pope said that he was moving ahead with improving Vatican governance, including with the committee of eight cardinals that he named in April. "I am very disorganized, I have never been good at this," Francis is quoted as saying. "But the cardinals of the commission will move it forward."

In its statement, CLAR added that it had not made a recording of Francis' remarks, but that those present, a half-dozen men and women, had written a summary of his points for their personal use. "It's clear that based on this, one cannot attribute with certainty to the Holy Father singular expressions in the text, but just the general sense," the statement said.

The summary also quoted the pope as saying that he had not imagined he would be elected pope. He said he had come to Rome "only with the necessary clothes, I washed them at night, and suddenly this ... And I did not have any chance!" the summary read. "In the London betting houses I was in 44th place, look at that, the one who bet on me won a lot, of course...! This does not come from me," he added, indicating it had been God's will.

GAIA PIANIGIANI contributed reporting.

Pope Replaces Conservative U.S. Cardinal on Influential Vatican Committee

BY JIM YARDLEY AND JASON HOROWITZ | DEC. 16, 2013

ROME — Pope Francis moved on Monday against a conservative American cardinal who has been an outspoken critic of abortion and same-sex marriage, by replacing him on a powerful Vatican committee with another American who is less identified with the culture wars within the Roman Catholic Church.

The pope's decision to remove Cardinal Raymond L. Burke from the Congregation for Bishops was taken by church experts to be a signal that Francis is willing to disrupt the Vatican establishment in order to be more inclusive.

Even so, many saw the move less as an effort to change doctrine on specific social issues than an attempt to bring a stylistic and pastoral consistency to the church's leadership.

"He is saying that you don't need to be a conservative to become a bishop," said Alberto Melloni, the director of the John XXIII Foundation for Religious Studies in Bologna, Italy, a liberal Catholic research institute. "He wants good bishops, regardless of how conservative or liberal they are."

Cardinal Burke, who came to the Vatican in 2008 after serving as archbishop of St. Louis, is a favorite of many conservative Catholics in the United States for his upholding of church rites and traditions favored by Pope Benedict XVI. Cardinal Burke's preference for the long train of billowing red silk known as cappa magna, and other such vestments, has, however, made him seem out of step with Francis, who has made it clear through example that he prefers more humble attire.

Last week, Cardinal Burke also seemed to create more substantive daylight between himself and the pope, giving an interview in which he raised concerns about comments by Francis that the church should reduce the focus on abortion and same-sex marriage.

"One gets the impression, or it's interpreted this way in the media, that he thinks we're talking too much about abortion, too much about the integrity of marriage as between one man and one woman," Cardinal Burke said of the pope in an interview with EWTN, a Catholic broadcaster. "But we can never talk enough about that."

Since his election as pope in March, Francis has received glowing news media coverage and widespread adulation from the faithful for putting a kinder, more inclusive face on a global institution that had been widely perceived as out of touch. He has expressed an intention to reorganize and overhaul the Roman Curia, the bureaucracy that governs the church.

Cardinal Burke still serves as the prefect of the Vatican's highest canonical court, but analysts say his removal from the Congregation for Bishops will sharply reduce his influence, especially over personnel changes in American churches.

"The Congregation for Bishops is the most important congregation in the Vatican," said the Rev. Thomas J. Reese, a Jesuit priest and the author of "Inside the Vatican: The Politics and Organization of the Catholic Church."

"It decides who are going to be the bishops all over the world," he added. "This is what has the most direct impact on the life of the local church."

To replace Cardinal Burke, Francis chose Cardinal Donald Wuerl of Washington, an ideological moderate with a deep knowledge of the Vatican but also with pastoral experience. Father Reese noted that Cardinal Burke had been a leader of American bishops arguing that Catholic politicians who support abortion rights should be barred from receiving communion, while Cardinal Wuerl had taken an opposite tack.

"That certainly is in line with the pope, who has said that communion is not a reward for being good," Father Reese said. "It is a sacrament of healing to help people."

The pope also removed Cardinal Justin Rigali, the former archbishop of Philadelphia, from the Congregation for Bishops. From his committee post, Cardinal Rigali has long been a crucial player in shaping the American hierarchy. He stepped down as archbishop of Philadelphia amid a scandal over his handling of priest abuse cases there.

And Francis reconfirmed the congregational posting for Cardinal William J. Levada, a former prefect of the Congregation for the Doctrine of the Faith. Like Cardinal Wuerl, Cardinal Levada is considered a moderate.

Some recent appointments have disheartened liberals within the church, particularly the pope's choice in October to approve the Rev. Leonard Blair as the archbishop of Hartford. He was central in a doctrinal investigation that reprimanded a group of American nuns who were deemed to have drifted from church teaching.

Many church observers saw the hand of Cardinal Burke in that selection, as they did in the appointment of Salvatore J. Cordileone, an outspoken opponent of same-sex marriage, as archbishop of San Francisco.

In an interview in Washington last week, Cardinal Wuerl suggested that the pope was altering the way the bishops' congregation functioned. For example, Francis is already surveying a broader range of bishops than those in the congregation, the cardinal said.

"When it comes to future bishops, he is asking a number of sources," he said.

Asked whether all of the pope's changes mattered if Cardinal Burke still had such influence in appointing bishops, Cardinal Wuerl smiled.

"Don't we have to give this pope time?" he said.

JIM YARDLEY reported from Rome, and **JASON HOROWITZ** from Washington. **GAIA PIANIGIANI** contributed reporting from Rome, and **LAURIE GOODSTEIN** from New York.

Ten Centuries Later, a Pope and Knights Do Battle

BY JASON HOROWITZ | JAN. 28, 2017

ROME — It began as a fight over staffing. Then came a dispute about condoms, followed by papal concerns about Freemasons. Now it has become a full-scale proxy war between Pope Francis and the Vatican traditionalists who oppose him, with the battleground being a Renaissance palace flanked by Jimmy Choo and Hermès storefronts on Via dei Condotti, Rome's most exclusive street.

The palace is the headquarters of the Knights of Malta, the medieval Roman Catholic order. For months, an ugly, if quiet, spat over staffing simmered behind the order's walls before spilling across the Tiber River to the Vatican, setting off a back-and-forth between the two camps. Francis and his lieutenants sent angry letters. The Knights ignored them, claiming sovereignty.

This past week, the dispute finally blew up. Fed up, Francis took the extraordinary steps of demanding the resignation of the order's leader — a decision the Knights officially accepted Saturday — and announcing that a papal delegate would step in.

Conservatives promptly denounced what they called an illegal annexation and ideological purging by a power-obsessed pontiff, while liberal observers saw the whole episode as resulting from an act of subterfuge by the pope's most public critic within the Vatican hierarchy, Cardinal Raymond Burke, an American.

A seemingly obscure intra-Catholic squabble had erupted into an unexpected shock to the church with ideological fault lines running to the top of the Vatican.

"The Vatican is a thing built of tradition," said John Thavis, the author of "The Vatican Diaries" and a veteran church analyst, "and once those traditional parts start feuding with each other, that is a dangerous sign."

Francis remains one of the world's most popular figures, but the

"It sends a message to the rest of the Catholic world that if you try to stand for orthodoxy in the church, you are going to be sent away," Mr. Hichborn said. "And the people pushing for heterodoxy will be put in power."

What was not up for debate was that, in the Vatican, Francis gets his way.

At the order's headquarters, a stately wooden mailbox hangs on the doorman's wall. The three top slots are reserved for the order's top three officials. On Wednesday morning, Mr. Boeselager's name had been erased. Mr. Festing's would soon be gone.

The third slot belonged to the order's interim leader, Grand Commander Ludwig Hoffmann von Rumerstein. But only, a Vatican statement made clear, "pending the appointment of the papal delegate."

The Pope Causes More Pain for Priests' Victims

EDITORIAL | BY THE NEW YORK TIMES | JAN. 19, 2018

POPE FRANCIS ARRIVED in Chile with the right message: He was "pained and ashamed," he said on Tuesday, about the irreparable damage abusive priests have inflicted on minors. Yet he refused to meet with victims of the country's most nefarious sexual abuser, and when pressed about his support of a bishop linked to that priest, he dismissed the accusations as slander.

For all his professions of horror at the revelations about predatory priests whose activities were covered up by the hierarchy — and for all his other admirably enlightened and pastoral actions — it seems the pope has yet to fully appreciate that the abuse of minors is not simply a matter of a few deviant priests protected by overzealous prelates but of his church's acceptance of a horrible violation of a most sacred trust: that of a devout and questioning youth and a spiritual guide.

Acknowledging and regretting the damage is not enough. If the Catholic Church is ever to lift the deep stain of child sex abuse, the pope must take every opportunity to reject not only clear violations but also the slightest appearance of tolerance for such behavior.

He missed that opportunity by attending the funeral last month for Cardinal Bernard Law, the powerful former archbishop of Boston who resigned after revelations that he protected abusive priests for years and became, in effect, the image of a hierarchy that concealed and thereby enabled sexual abuse. He missed it in the failure of the Vatican so far to appoint a new Pontifical Commission for the Protection of Minors after the commissioners' terms expired in December.

And Pope Francis missed it again in Chile. One of Latin America's most staunchly Catholic countries, Chile had been shaken by revelations about the sexual crimes of Fernando Karadima, once one of Chile's most respected and influential priests. It took years for the church to act on complaints about him, but a Vatican investigation in 2011 finally found Father Karadima guilty of sexual abuse and restricted him to a life of isolated penitence. A Chilean judge later determined that the allegations against the priest were truthful, but the statute of limitations had expired.

Among those accused of turning a blind eye to Father Karadima's behavior was a priest and longtime member of Father Karadima's entourage, Juan Barros Madrid. Yet Pope Francis made him a bishop in 2015 and, despite protests from victims of Father Karadima and from many priests and laypeople in the diocese, Bishop Barros participated in the pope's official ceremonies in Chile. When reporters raised the subject on Thursday, Pope Francis answered sharply that there was "not one single piece of evidence" against the bishop. "It is all slander," he declared. "Is that clear?"

No, it is not clear.

Victims of sexual abuse may have only their tortured memories as evidence, and these have been dismissed for far too long as slander by a hierarchy intent on protecting the church's reputation. Pope Francis has repeatedly pledged action to end the abuse and the cover-up, and the church has come a long way. But too often he and his church raise doubts that they're fully committed.

Pope Francis, After Criticism, Sends Sex Crimes Investigator to Chile

BY JASON HOROWITZ | JAN. 30, 2018

ROME — When it comes to sexual abuse in the Roman Catholic Church, supporters of Pope Francis are hoping that if indeed he was blind, now he sees.

Francis on Tuesday dispatched the Vatican's leading sex crimes investigator to Chile, days after the pope's vigorous, repeated and potentially disastrous defense of Bishop Juan Barros Madrid, who is accused of protecting the country's most notorious pedophile priest.

"As a result of some information received recently regarding the case," the Vatican said in a statement on Tuesday, the church will send to Chile the Maltese Archbishop Charles Scicluna, who has been called the Vatican's Eliot Ness in fighting clerical sex abuse. There, the statement continued, he will "hear those who have expressed the desire to provide elements in their possession."

By elements in their possession, the Vatican apparently means the testimony and painful stories of victims that the pope had previously dismissed as slanderous accusations.

The pope's belief of a powerful bishop over victims outraged advocates for the survivors of sexual abuse both outside and inside the church. The outcry over the pope's blind spot to clerical sexual abuse, and his tin ear to the anguish of its victims, threatened to indelibly stain the pontificate of a usually politically astute pope.

The pope's supporters on Tuesday quickly embraced the decision as an important course correction.

"It is a positive development in so far that it makes clear that the Holy See is interested to learn from and hear the testimonies of witnesses," said the Rev. Hans Zollner, who served as a member of the Pontifical Commission for the Protection of Minors. It was clear

Francis had "listened to the questions that some journalists have put to him," Father Zollner added. "He has learned from the reactions."

But victims in Chile said that while the news was welcome, they hoped it was not a public relations gambit.

"Nobody has said anything to us," said Juan Carlos Cruz, a Chilean who says he was sexually abused by the Rev. Fernando Karadima. He has said that Bishop Barros witnessed the abuse and did nothing about it.

He said that he would be willing to testify, as victims have been doing to church law tribunals since 2005, and added, "We are encouraged."

Francis' trip to Chile in mid-January was overshadowed by his brusque remarks to a Chilean reporter that the claims against Bishop Barros amounted to "slander." The pope said he would weigh in on the matter if there were "proof" against the bishop.

Cardinal Sean O'Malley, the archbishop of Boston and the leader of the pope's commission on the protection of minors, called the pope's remarks "a source of great pain for survivors" that relegated them "to discredited exile."

In a clumsy attempt at damage control, the pope made a contradictory statement on the flight back to Rome. He apologized for demanding proof from alleged victims, saying that the word was insensitive, but then reiterated that there was no "evidence" against the bishop, who he again said was the victim of slander.

Some victims of Father Karadima, a powerful priest convicted by the Vatican in 2011 for sexually abusing minors, have accused Bishop Barros of standing by as the priest kissed and abused them in the El Bosque Catholic parish.

On the plane, Francis said he had twice refused to accept the resignation of Bishop Barros, and in January 2015 he moved the bishop from leading Chile's military ordinariate to the diocese of Osorno. The installation fractured the faithful and clergy of the city, with many opposing a bishop they considered complicit in sexual abuse.

The pope's response mystified observers and vexed his supporters. Possible explanations tumbled out. Was he getting bad advice from his cardinal advisers? Was he protecting a friend? Was he a member of a Vatican faction that believes in "zero tolerance" or one that considers the abuse issue finished business? Was the pope, someone who faced accusations of supporting a violent regime as a cardinal in Argentina, loath to give into public pressure?

Tuesday's statement suggested that public pressure had forced the pope to act and that far from infallible, Francis had perhaps spoken in Chile without knowing what he was talking about.

By contrast, Bishop Scicluna has in the last decade emerged as the Vatican prelate who most gets it when it comes to the issue of sexual abuse.

Bishop Scicluna, who declined to comment for this article, acted as a prosecutor during his time at the Congregation for the Doctrine of the Faith under Pope Benedict XVI. He took on the powerful Rev. Marcial Maciel Degollado of Mexico, the founder of the influential Legionaries of Christ, who was considered untouchable because of his close ties to and protection under Pope John Paul II.

For years, Vatican prelates dismissed the accusations of Father Degollado's victims as slander, but Bishop Scicluna listened to them and, after John Paul's death, convinced the Vatican that Father Degollado had abused seminarians in his own order.

Benedict sentenced Father Degollado to a life of penance and prayer in 2006. Father Degollado died in 2008, and was later shown to have been a serial molester who fathered children by two women.

Archbishop Scicluna subsequently explained that Benedict, previously John Paul's chief doctrinal watchdog, had undergone a conversion on the issue as he sat at his desk reading horrific dossier after horrific dossier.

Advocates for Francis hope that Archbishop Scicluna will now figure in opening up the eyes of another pontiff.

“It is good that he has now looked anew and taken this step,” Marie Collins, an abuse survivor who last year resigned in frustration from the pope’s Pontifical Commission for the Protection of Minors, wrote on Twitter.

Despite Francis’ promises to rid the church of abuse, many Vatican watchers consider him far less effective than Benedict, who removed many priests. Francis has mostly disappointed those who hoped he would bring accountability to the church hierarchy.

Last year, he instead recalled a Vatican diplomat accused of possession of child pornography back to Rome, despite efforts by the American authorities to strip the priest of his immunity. Last month, the terms of the members of the Vatican commission on abuse expired. The pope has called the delay in restarting the commission “normal.”

Father Zollner, himself a member of that commission, said he had witnessed meetings between Francis and victims. In Chile, he said, the pope, like any leader, found himself in an “ethical dilemma” in which he wanted to believe victims but needed to be sure that their allegations were true.

And given the intense attention on the issue now, he said, Archbishop Scicluna’s mission to get to the bottom of it will be especially challenging.

“He needs to get as much evidence as possible now,” he said. “One way or the other.”

Pope Francis Is Beloved. His Papacy Might Be a Disaster.

OPINION | BY ROSS DOUTHAT | MARCH 16, 2018

THE CONVERSATION has become predictable. A friendly acquaintance — a neighbor, a fellow parent, our real estate agent — asks about my work. I say I've been writing a book about the pope, and the acquaintance smiles and nods and says "Isn't he so wonderful?" or, "That must be an inspiring thing," or, "I have a friend who would love to read it." And then eventually I find myself saying, uncomfortably, "Well, they should know that it's not entirely favorable."

A pause, puzzled and slightly crestfallen. "But you're writing about the nice pope?"

The consistency of these exchanges is a testament to the great achievement of Pope Francis' five years on the papal throne. He leads a church that spent the prior decade embroiled in a grisly sex abuse scandal, occupies an office often regarded as a medieval relic, and operates in a media environment in which traditional religion generally, and Roman Catholicism especially, are often covered with a mix of cluelessness and malice.

And yet in a remarkably short amount of time — from the first days after his election, really — the former Jorge Bergoglio has made his pontificate a vessel for religious hopes that many of his admirers didn't realize or remember that they had.

Some of this admiration reflects the specific controversies he's stirred within the church, the theological risks he's taken in pushing for changes that liberal Westerners tend to assume Catholicism must eventually accept — shifts on sexual morality above all, plus a general liberalization in the hierarchy and the church.

But when people say, "He makes me want to believe again," as a lapsed-Catholic journalist said to me during one of these awkward "What do you have against Pope Francis?" conversations, they aren't

The risks of the Chinese gamble are already apparent in the weirdly sycophantic language that Francis' allies have used toward the Communist regime, and their eagerness to reassure Beijing that unlike, say, American evangelicals, Rome would never take the threatening step of mixing religion and politics.

If current trends continue, China could have one of the world's largest Christian populations by this century's end, and this population is already heavily evangelical; indeed, the Vatican's desire for a deal with Beijing is influenced by the fact that a divided Chinese Catholicism is being outcompeted for converts.

But if that deal permanently links the Roman church with a corrupt and fated regime, Francis will have ceded the moral authority earned by persecuted generations, and ceded the Chinese future to those Christian churches, evangelical especially, that are less eager to flatter and cajole their persecutors.

The gamble on an Anglican approach to faith and morals is even more high-risk — as Anglicanism's own schisms well attest. The pope's "new paradigm" has defused the immediate threat of schism by maintaining a studious ambiguity whenever challenged. But it will ensure that the church's factions, already polarized and feuding, grow ever more apart. And it implies a rupture (or, if you favor it, a breakthrough) in the church's understanding of how its teachings can and cannot change — one less dramatic in immediate effect than the reforms of the Second Vatican Council, but ultimately more far-reaching in its implications for Catholicism.

Francis' inner circle is convinced that such a revolution is what the Holy Spirit wants — that the attempts by John Paul II and Benedict to maintain continuity between the church before and after Vatican II ended up choking off renewal.

They are right that the John Paul II paradigm was fraught with flaws and tensions; the ease with which Francis has reopened debates that conservatives considered closed has testified to that. But this pope has not just exposed tensions; he has heightened them, encouraging sweeping ambitions among his allies and pushing disillusioned conservatives toward traditionalism. Like certain imprudent medieval popes, Francis has pressed papal authority to its limits — theological this time, not temporal, but no less dangerous for that.

All of this makes for interesting copy for those of us who write about the church. Truces are unsatisfying and instability is exciting and theological civil wars can be worth waging. But there is no sign as yet that Francis' liberalization is bringing his lapsed-Catholic admirers back to the pews; from Germany to Australia to his native Latin America, the church's institutional decline continues. And sustaining a for-the-time-being Catholicism, as his immediate predecessors did, is not an achievement to be lightly dismissed. Whereas accelerating division when your office is charged with maintaining unity and continuity is a serious business — especially when the eventual resolution is so bafflingly difficult to envision or predict.

It is wise for Francis' Catholic critics to temper our presumption, always, by acknowledging the possibility that we are misled or missing something, and that this story could end with this popular pope proven to be visionary and heroic.

But to choose a path that might have only two destinations — hero or heretic — is also an act of presumption, even for a pope. Especially for a pope.

Adapted from "To Change the Church: Pope Francis and the Future of Catholicism," forthcoming from Simon and Schuster March 2018.
ROSS DOUTHAT is an Op-Ed columnist for The New York Times.

Francis, the Anti-Strongman

OPINION | BY PAUL ELIE | MARCH 24, 2018

VATICAN CITY — One recent Friday evening, Pope Francis presided over a penitential service at St. Peter's. After the Gospel was read he strode beneath the great dome and knelt at a wooden booth, while other Catholics did likewise throughout the basilica. "I am a sinner," he had said shortly after his election in 2013, and five years later the self-description still holds: Before going into the booth to listen as others confessed their sins, he confessed his own.

In recent centuries, the pope has been both symbol and cipher for an authoritarian ruler. As Western governments became more expressive of the will of the governed, the leader of the Roman Catholic Church has been seen, by contrast, as a figure vested in bulletproof pre-modern absolutes, immune to electoral or popular pressures, accountable to God alone.

So it's striking that in our time, Pope Francis has emerged as a counterweight to authoritarian rule, a pope who has set the office he holds in symbolic opposition to would-be autocrats.

The age of the strongman is at hand: Xi Jinping in China, Vladimir Putin in Russia, Viktor Orban in Hungary and Donald Trump in the United States all disdain checks and balances, the independent press and other forces that might counter a self-determined chief executive.

In these circumstances, Pope Francis has emerged as the anti-strongman. His choice of name evoked Francis of Assisi, humble patron saint of the poor. His decision to live in the Santa Marta guesthouse rather than the Vatican Palace suggested his essential simplicity. Paying his hotel bill in Rome, carrying his own briefcase onto Shepherd One: Here was a pope with both feet on the ground.

Those gestures also signaled his wish to unhitch the papacy from the office's authoritarian legacy. The name Francis (never before chosen by a pope) placed him outside the lineage of his roman-numeraled, monarchical predecessors. Setting up in the guesthouse kept him clear of the papacy's history of worldly power through rule of the Papal States. Paying his hotel bill suggested that even a potentate doesn't get a free ride.

Francis took office at a time of unprecedented change for the papacy. Benedict's resignation in February 2013 — the first by a pope in 598 years — altered the power structure of the Vatican overnight. Now that it can no longer be assumed a pope will rule for life, the Vatican is less like an absolute monarchy than a coalition government in which politicking is out in the open and the pope must hold factions together.

Francis has embraced this new openness: appointing a group of consulting cardinals, and actually consulting them; holding a papal synod focused on discussion more than conclusions; answering hard questions unguardedly; and taking his strongest stand on the problem of environmental degradation.

Even as they grant that he was elected to shake up the constricted Vatican bureaucracy, his critics see his approach as that of a stealthy revolutionary or a reckless agent of disruption. In fact, Francis' exercise of the papal role reflects the Jesuit practice of discernment, which involves waiting, listening, letting competing options for action emerge, and choosing one after prayer and internal deliberation.

The group of advisory cardinals is significant because it belies the supposed solitary autonomy of papal decision-making and incorporates cardinals from places long thought remote from power: Santiago, Chile, and Mumbai, India, as well as Munich and Boston. The group's members are compromised figures whose blind spots are often akin to Francis' own. But it is a significant step that such a body exists at all.

The 2015 synod on marriage and the family, judged a debacle by many, is better understood as an instance of soft power in action. By calling the synod, Francis signaled that the issues surrounding Catholic teaching on marriage are not closed to further Vatican discussion — in sharp contrast to the "Rome has spoken" approach of his predecessors. Then Francis set out to point the synod discussions in a progressive direction on the issue of whether divorced-and-remarried Catholics in certain countries may receive communion at Mass. Traditionalists accused Francis of flirting with heresy.

Of necessity, the process was unruly. But discussions were had, and cardinals who opposed Francis were heard — because Francis let them be heard. He gave a closing speech thick with exasperation, replaced some resistant curial officials and demoted the hostile American Cardinal Raymond Burke — but he set aside the most far-reaching proposals about marriage and family for a future time, meanwhile keeping the discussion open.

Francis has acted on his conviction that Catholic faith is less about the use of power to shape the social order — the stuff of present strongmen and past popes — than about straightforward efforts of kindness and generosity.

While John Paul forged a relationship with Opus Dei — the strict and secretive movement with roots in the postwar Spain of Francisco

EMILIANO PONZI

Franco — Francis is at ease with the Community of Sant'Egidio, founded in Rome during the student uprisings of 1968 and now present in 70 countries, working with the poor, migrants, the elderly and people with AIDS. With its members, Francis has acted like a 21st-century Christian who happens to be pope: washing the feet of Muslim men and women on Holy Thursday, airlifting Syrians out of the Lesbos refugee camp on the papal plane and instituting a shelter for homeless people inside the Vatican.

Francis could serve as pope for another year, or five or 10. The test of his soft power in the coming years will be its encounter with hard power. Will he issue an encyclical on migration and the demonizing of the immigrant "other"? As he seeks openings for the church in seething Russia and rising China, will he address those countries' human rights violations, opposing authoritarianism with the authority of the Gospel? Possibly — but not certainly. Traditionalists in the Vatican are insisting that Francis would do better not to engage with intransigent leaders and intractable problems at all. And Francis' record is frankly poor in some areas. On priestly sexual abuse, for example, he has acted like a highhanded cleric of old instead of taking firm, clear action.

Symbolically, the papacy is meant to be a "contrast structure" to worldly forms of authority. Too often, it has been such a structure in the wrong ways: crabbed, self-protecting, aloof and denunciatory. Five years into his pontificate, Francis is no small-d democrat, no faultless leader — and no perfect pope. And yet in this pope, our upside-down age has a leader whose approach and example stand as reminders of what the sensitive exercise of power can look like.

PAUL ELIE, the author of "The Life You Save May Be Your Own" and "Reinventing Bach," is a senior fellow at Georgetown's Berkley Center for Religion, Peace and World Affairs.

Catholic Priests Abused 1,000 Children in Pennsylvania, Report Says

BY LAURIE GOODSTEIN AND SHARON OTTERMAN | AUG. 14, 2018

BISHOPS AND OTHER LEADERS of the Roman Catholic Church in Pennsylvania covered up child sexual abuse by more than 300 priests over a period of 70 years, persuading victims not to report the abuse and law enforcement not to investigate it, according to a searing report issued by a grand jury on Tuesday.

The report, which covered six of the state's eight Catholic dioceses and found more than 1,000 identifiable victims, is the broadest examination yet by a government agency in the United States of child sexual abuse in the Catholic Church. The report said there are likely thousands more victims whose records were lost or who were too afraid to come forward.

It catalogs horrific instances of abuse: a priest who raped a young girl in the hospital after she had her tonsils out; a victim tied up and whipped with leather straps by a priest; and another priest who was allowed to stay in ministry after impregnating a young girl and arranging for her to have an abortion.

The sexual abuse scandal has shaken the Catholic Church for more than 15 years, ever since explosive allegations emerged out of Boston in 2002. But even after paying billions of dollars in settlements and adding new prevention programs, the church has been dogged by a scandal that is now reaching its highest ranks. The Pennsylvania report comes soon after the resignation of Cardinal Theodore E. McCarrick, the former archbishop of Washington, who is accused of sexually abusing young priests and seminarians, as well as minors.

"Despite some institutional reform, individual leaders of the church have largely escaped public accountability," the grand jury wrote. "Priests were raping little boys and girls, and the men of God who were responsible for them not only did nothing; they hid it all. For decades."

The grand jury said that while some accused priests were removed from ministry, the church officials who protected them remained in office or even got promotions. One bishop named in the report as vouching for an abusive priest was Cardinal Donald Wuerl, now the archbishop of Washington. "Until that changes, we think it is too early to close the book on the Catholic Church sex scandal," the jury wrote.

The report is unlikely to lead to new criminal charges or civil lawsuits under the current law because the statute of limitations has expired. Only two of the cases in the report so far have led to criminal charges.

In statements released on Tuesday, Pennsylvania's Catholic bishops called for prayers for victims and for the church, promised greater openness and said that measures instituted in recent years were already making the church safer.

But several bishops, including Bishop David A. Zubik of Pittsburgh, rejected the idea the church had concealed abuse.

"There was no cover-up going on," Bishop Zubik said in a news conference on Tuesday. "I think that it's important to be able to state that. We have over the course of the last 30 years, for sure, been transparent about everything that has in fact been transpiring."

Church officials followed a "playbook for concealing the truth," the grand jury said, minimizing the abuse by using words like "inappropriate contact" instead of "rape"; assigning priests untrained in sexual abuse cases to investigate their colleagues; and not informing the community of the real reasons behind removing an accused priest.

"Tell his parishioners that he is on 'sick leave,' or suffering from 'nervous exhaustion.' Or say nothing at all," the report said.

Attorney General Josh Shapiro, whose office initiated the investigation, said in a news conference, "They protected their institution at all costs. As the grand jury found, the church showed a complete disdain for victims."

He said that the cover-up by senior church officials "stretched in some cases all the way up to the Vatican."

No other state has seen more grand jury investigations of abuses in the church than Pennsylvania, where about one of every four residents is Catholic and the local attorneys general have been particularly responsive to victims. Previous grand juries examined the dioceses of Philadelphia and Altoona-Johnstown; the new report covers the rest of the state.

Mr. Shapiro was surrounded on Tuesday by about 20 abuse victims and their family members, who gasped and wept when he revealed that one priest had abused five sisters in the same family, including one girl beginning when she was 18 months old.

Some victims said in interviews that they were relieved to finally be heard and to have their perpetrators publicly named.

"I had gone to two bishops with allegations over five years, and they ignored and downplayed my allegations," said the Rev. James Faluszczak, an Erie priest on extended leave who was abused as a child and who testified before the grand jury. "It's that very management of secrets that has given cover to predators."

For others, it was too little, too late. Frances Samber, whose brother Michael was abused by a priest in Pittsburgh and committed suicide in 2010, said, "It's good that the public sees this, but where is the justice? What do you do about it? Why aren't these people in prison?"

There has been no comprehensive measurement of the full scope of child sexual abuse in the Catholic Church in the United States, though some have tried. American abuse survivors have pushed for years for the government to undertake a nationwide inquiry similar to the one conducted in Australia, where a royal commission spent four years examining the sexual abuse of children by a variety of religious and civic institutions, including the Catholic Church.

There have been 10 previous reports by grand juries and attorneys general in the United States, according to the research and advocacy group BishopAccountability.org, but those examined single dioceses or counties.

The Pennsylvania grand jury report lands as the sex abuse scandal in the church has reached a new stage, with calls to discipline bishops who sexually abused younger priests and seminarians, or who have covered up for abusive colleagues.

Catholics are calling for independent investigations into why Cardinal McCarrick was advanced up the hierarchy despite warnings to his superiors in Rome and fellow bishops that he had molested seminarians and young priests. Cardinal McCarrick resigned in July over allegations of sexually abusing minors, but since then priests in the diocese of Lincoln, Nebraska, and seminarians in Boston and elsewhere have publicly accused their superiors of turning a blind eye to sexual misconduct.

The Pennsylvania grand jury met for two years, reviewed 500,000 documents from dioceses' secret archives, and heard testimony from dozens of victims and the bishop of Erie. The report covers the dioceses of Allentown, Erie, Greensburg, Harrisburg, Pittsburgh and Scranton. Two of the dioceses — Greensburg and Harrisburg — tried to quash the grand jury investigation last year, but later backed off that stance.

The report lists each of the accused priests and documents how they were sent from parish to parish, and even sometimes out of state. The grand jury said that while the list is long, "we don't think we got them all." The report added, "We feel certain that many victims never came forward, and that the dioceses did not create written records every single time they heard something about abuse."

In the Greensburg diocese, the Rev. John Sweeney was charged by the attorney general's office with sexually abusing a boy in the early 1990s. Father Sweeney pleaded guilty this month and awaits sentencing. In the Erie diocese, the Rev. David Poulson was arrested in May and charged with sexually assaulting a boy for eight years, starting at age 8. Father Poulson has yet to enter a plea.

The Pennsylvania State Legislature has so far resisted calls to lift the statute of limitations, which has prevented childhood victims from filing civil lawsuits against the church after they turn 30. For many victims, it has taken decades to gain the courage to speak about the abuse, long past when the law would allow them to sue.

The grand jury and the attorney general strongly recommended that the statute of limitations be extended in civil and criminal cases. They recommended opening a temporary "window" that would permit older victims to file civil lawsuits against perpetrators, and the church.

The church has lobbied against any change to the statute or to open such a window, its efforts led by Bishop Ronald W. Gainer of Harrisburg, president of the Pennsylvania Catholic Conference. But abuse survivors and advocates say that in September they plan to begin a fresh campaign to press lawmakers and Bishop Gainer to drop their opposition.

"If this doesn't start a serious debate on the elimination of the statute of limitation, there's something seriously wrong with my fellow Pennsylvanians," said Shaun Dougherty, now 48, who testified before the Altoona-Johnstown grand jury about being abused by a priest for three years starting at age 10.

About two dozen people named in the report petitioned the court to have their names redacted from it.

In the news conference, Mr. Shapiro, the attorney general, described the "intense legal battle" that played out over the last several months as some people named in the report appealed to the Pennsylvania Supreme Court to block its release.

"They wanted to cover up the cover-up," he said.

Mr. Shapiro said his office would continue to fight for a full version of the report to be released with no redactions.

One example of a cover-up detailed in the report concerns the Rev. Ernest Paone, a priest who was caught molesting boys and using guns with young children in Pittsburgh. A fellow pastor intervened in 1962 to stop the police from arresting him. The district attorney at the time, Robert Masters, wrote to the diocese in 1964 to say that he had halted his investigation of the case "in order to prevent unfavorable publicity" for the diocese.

In testimony before the grand jury, Mr. Masters said that he had wanted the church's support for his political career.

Father Paone was relocated successively to Los Angeles, San Diego and Reno in the following years, with Pittsburgh's bishops attesting to his fitness as a priest. Among those bishops was Cardinal Wuerl, now the archbishop of Washington. He accepted Father Paone's resignation from ministry in good standing in 2003, allowing him to collect his pension.

Cardinal Wuerl released a letter to his priests on Monday, saying that while the grand jury report would be "critical of some of my actions, I believe the report also confirms that I acted with diligence, with concern for the survivors and to prevent future acts of abuse."

As of Tuesday, all six of the dioceses covered by the report had released the names of priests with allegations against them.

Bishop Gainer in Harrisburg recently ordered that the names of accused priests and of bishops who mishandled abuse cases be taken down from all church buildings in the diocese.

The report says that one of the victims who had testified before the grand jury tried to commit suicide while they were deliberating.

"From her hospital bed, she asked for one thing," the grand jury wrote in the report, "that we finish our work and tell the world what really happened."

Pope Francis Long Knew of Cardinal's Abuse and Must Resign, Archbishop Says

BY JASON HOROWITZ | AUG. 26, 2018

DUBLIN — On the final day of Pope Francis' mission to Ireland, as he issued wrenching apologies for clerical sex abuse scandals, a former top Vatican diplomat claimed in a letter published on Sunday that the pope himself had joined top Vatican officials in covering up the abuses and called for his resignation.

The letter, a bombshell written by Carlo Maria Viganò, the former top Vatican diplomat in the United States and a staunch critic of the pope's, seemed timed to do more than simply derail Francis' uphill efforts to win back the Irish faithful, who have turned away from the church in large numbers.

Its unsubstantiated allegations and personal attacks amounted to an extraordinary public declaration of war against Francis' papacy at perhaps its most vulnerable moment, intended to unseat a pope whose predecessor, Benedict XVI, was the first pontiff to resign in nearly 600 years.

Archbishop Viganò claimed that the Vatican hierarchy was complicit in covering up accusations that Cardinal Theodore McCarrick had sexually abused seminarians and that Pope Francis knew about the abuses by the now-disgraced American prelate years before they became public. Yet, the letter contended, Francis did not punish the cardinal, but instead empowered him to help choose powerful American bishops.

In a news conference on the papal plane back to Rome late Sunday evening, Francis was asked whether there was any truth to the claim that Archbishop Viganò had personally informed him in 2013 of Cardinal McCarrick's history of abuse. He was also asked whether Benedict had sanctioned the American cardinal, as the letter also claimed.

The pope did not deny it, but sidestepped the questions by insisting he would not dignify them with a response.

"I will not say a single word about this," he said. "I believe the statement speaks for itself. And you have the sufficient journalistic ability to make your conclusions. It's an act of trust."

The 7,000-word attack on Francis' allies in the Vatican, published early Sunday Dublin time by several conservative Catholic outlets antagonistic to the pope, represented a steep escalation in the long-standing, and increasingly caustic, rivalries within the church.

Factions have battled over the direction the church has gone under Francis, with conservatives, especially some American cardinals and bishops, warning that his pastoral and inclusive approach and emphasis on social issues dilute church doctrine and pose a mortal threat to the future of the faith.

Already on Sunday afternoon, the battle was being joined.

Cardinal Blase J. Cupich, the archbishop of Chicago, who is aligned with Francis and was a target of Archbishop Viganò's letter, said in a phone interview that he suspected English speakers had helped Archbishop Viganò write the letter. He called the pope "a man of integrity."

"If he makes a mistake, he admits it," Cardinal Cupich said. "That's why I'm convinced this is something that he is going to respond to in an appropriate way."

Cardinal Cupich also said the timing of the letter raised questions.

"I'd have to leave it up to him to ask him why he timed the release of this at this moment, particularly if he considered this information so very critical and important," the cardinal said.

Archbishop Charles J. Chaput of Philadelphia, a leading conservative voice in the Catholic Church, who according to the letter was disparaged by Francis, vouched for Archbishop Viganò's integrity in a statement from his spokesman.

The willingness of the pope and his allies to reach out to gay Catholics has infuriated conservatives, many of whom, like Archbishop Viganò, blame homosexuals for the sex abuse crisis. The pope has argued that the abuse is a symptom of a culture of privilege and imperviousness among priests who value the church's traditions over its parishioners.

Last month, Francis accepted the resignation of Cardinal McCarrick, the first such resignation in living memory, after The New York Times and other news outlets published accounts of the alleged abuse and an internal investigation by the American church deemed credible an accusation that he had sexually abused a minor.

Archbishop Viganò said that Benedict had already punished Cardinal McCarrick for his abuse of seminarians and priests. The archbishop writes that Benedict had banned the American cardinal from publicly celebrating Mass, from living in a seminary and from traveling to give lectures.

There is no public record of such a sanction, and the cardinal continued to celebrate Mass. And in 2012, Cardinal McCarrick joined bishops in the Vatican to sing happy birthday to Benedict as they presented him with a fresh strawberry-and-kiwi custard cake.

Cardinal Cupich said he was not aware of any restrictions that Pope Benedict put on Cardinal McCarrick, as Archbishop Viganò asserts.

"How can you have secret restrictions? What does that mean?" Cardinal Cupich said, adding that it would have been Archbishop Viganò's duty as nuncio to inform the American bishops of the restrictions. "Why didn't he tell us this?" he asked. "Why didn't he enforce it?"

Archbishop Viganò accused Francis of failing to apply the sanctions on Cardinal McCarrick and instead rehabilitating and entrusting him to help choose powerful American bishops, including Cardinal Cupich.

Archbishop Viganò despises many of those bishops, who now wield influence and promote Francis' pastoral approach, and he complained in the letter of being deprived of the voice typically given to a papal nuncio in choosing them. He targeted those bishops and cardinals by name, but saved his strongest fire for Francis.

"He knew from at least June 23, 2013, that McCarrick was a serial predator," Archbishop Viganò wrote.

"In this extremely dramatic moment for the universal Church," he wrote, "he must acknowledge his mistakes and, in keeping with the proclaimed principle of zero tolerance, Pope Francis must be the first to set a good example for cardinals and bishops who covered up McCarrick's abuses and resign along with all of them."

At a 2013 reception in the library of the Apostolic Palace in the Vatican shortly after Francis was elected pope, Archbishop Viganò was effusive with praise for him, saying his audience was "extremely nice, extremely warm."

But in the letter, he said he had received an icy reception from Francis. And he said the pope had told him on June 23, 2013: "The bishops in the United States must not be ideologized, they must not be right wing." Francis then added, according to Archbishop Viganò, that they must not be left wing, "and when I say left-wing, I mean homosexual." It was then, he said, that Francis asked his opinion of Cardinal McCarrick.

"Holy Father," Archbishop Viganò said he had responded, "I don't know if you know Cardinal McCarrick, but if you ask the Congregation for Bishops there is a dossier this thick about him. He corrupted generations of seminarians and priests, and Pope Benedict ordered him to withdraw to a life of prayer and penance."

Archbishop Viganò, who blames gays for the child abuse crisis that has destroyed the church's standing in many countries, dedicated entire sections of the letter to outing cardinals who he claims belong to what he characterizes as a pernicious "homosexual current" within the Vatican.

"These homosexual networks," he wrote, "which are now widespread in many dioceses, seminaries, religious orders, etc., act under the concealment of secrecy and lies with the power of octopus tentacles, and strangle innocent victims and priestly vocations, and are strangling the entire church."

Archbishop Viganò is no stranger to stirring trouble in the Vatican.

A cultural conservative born into a wealthy family in Varese, Italy, he received the title of archbishop from Pope John Paul II in 1992.

He later joined the church's diplomatic corps, one of the traditional sources of power in the Vatican, which gave him access to much of the information he alleges in the letter. In 2009, he was installed by Pope Benedict XVI as secretary of the governorate of Vatican City State, a position similar to mayor of Vatican City.

Benedict wanted him to enact government overhauls, but Archbishop Viganò's efforts in pursuit of that goal earned him powerful enemies.

In early 2011, hostile anonymous articles attacking Archbishop Viganò began appearing in the Italian news media, the bulletin board of Vatican power politics. Archbishop Viganò appealed to Benedict's second in command, Cardinal Tarcisio Bertone, who instead echoed the articles' complaints.

Those appeals and protests, later leaked by the pope's butler, became the heart of the church scandal known as VatiLeaks, which many church observers say contributed to Benedict XVI's resignation.

Francis removed Archbishop Viganò from his job as nuncio to the United States in 2016, in part for nearly ruining the pope's trip to the United States by giving papal face time to Kim Davis, the Kentucky clerk who refused to issue marriage licenses to same-sex couples.

Soon after his departure, a criminal investigation into an archbishop in Minneapolis-St. Paul revealed a memo that Archbishop Viganò had written in 2014 in an effort to suppress a church investigation into alleged homosexual activity by the Minnesota prelate, Archbishop John C. Nienstedt.

Since his return to Rome, Archbishop Viganò has associated with traditionalist Catholics deeply critical of Pope Francis.

Archbishop Viganò's letter, while especially inconvenient for the pope, who spent Sunday morning praying for abuse victims at a shrine in Knock, Ireland, also goes after a broad array of current and past Vatican officials and American prelates. He names all of them.

He said that his predecessors in the Vatican's embassy in Washington, now all deceased, knew about Cardinal McCarrick's alleged relationships with seminarians and priests and had reported it to the

Vatican, but that successive secretaries of state — Angelo Sodano, Cardinal Bertone and Pietro Parolin — did nothing.

Archbishop Viganò said that he had personally met with Cardinal McCarrick to remind him that he was under sanction during their first meeting after he arrived in the United States.

"The cardinal, muttering in a barely comprehensible way, admitted that he had perhaps made the mistake of sleeping in the same bed with some seminarians at his beach house," he writes.

After bumping into Cardinal McCarrick at the pope's residence in the Vatican, and listening to the American boast about his freedom to travel, Archbishop Viganò wrote, he contacted Cardinal Parolin, the secretary of state and top adviser to Francis, in April 2014 inquiring whether the sanctions were still in force.

He said that neither Cardinal Parolin nor a host of other Vatican officials had replied, but that when he had brought up the subject with Cardinal McCarrick's replacement in Washington, Cardinal Donald Wuerl, "it was immediately clear to me that he was fully aware of it."

Ed McFadden, a spokesman for Cardinal Wuerl, disputed that account on Sunday. "In spite of what Archbishop Viganò's memo indicates, Cardinal Wuerl did not receive any documentation or information during his time in Washington regarding any actions taken against Archbishop McCarrick," Mr. McFadden said.

Some survivors of clerical abuse called the allegations a distraction.

"This is infighting between curia factions that are exploiting the abuse crisis and victims of clergy sexual abuse as leverage in the struggle for church power," said Peter Isely, a survivor. "The sexual abuse crisis is not about whether a bishop is a liberal or a conservative. It is about protecting children."

The controversy over the allegations is expected to grow in coming days, especially as Francis has declined to deny it.

Instead on Sunday's flight, he blamed the media for promoting an "atmosphere of guilt" around suspected clerics and shared that until his visit he "had never heard" about Ireland's notorious mother and baby homes, where children were ripped away from unwed mothers.

He also sought to strike the same conciliatory tone that hundreds of thousands of faithful heard earlier in the day as he began a Mass at Phoenix Park in Dublin by explicitly asking forgiveness for the church's sins and abuse.

"Some members of the hierarchy didn't own up to these painful situations," he said at the Mass. "And kept silent."

ELIZABETH DIAS contributed reporting from Washington, and **LAURIE GOODSTEIN** from New York.

What Did Pope Francis Know?

OPINION | BY ROSS DOUTHAT | AUG. 28, 2018

The Catholic Church needs leaders who can purge corruption even among their own theological allies. The pope is failing that test.

DURING THE CATHOLIC CHURCH'S synod on the family in Rome in 2015, a rough-and-tumble affair in which Pope Francis pushed the assembled bishops to liberalize Catholic teaching on remarriage and divorce, one of the attendees, by the pope's own invitation, was the retired Belgian Cardinal Godfried Danneels.

Danneels was a natural pick in one sense: One of the church's prominent liberals, he had been part of a circle that supported Jorge Bergoglio in the run-up to his election as Francis, and in a synodal fight with conservative bishops, the pope needed all the allies he could get.

In another sense, though, Danneels was a wildly inappropriate choice, because at the conclusion of his career he was caught on tape trying to persuade a young victim of sex abuse not to go public with allegations against the victim's uncle, Bishop Roger Vangheluwe of Bruges, Belgium. For Pope Francis, who talked a good game about disciplining bishops for covering up sex abuse, hauling a cover-up artist out of retirement for a synod on the family was a statement that ideological loyalties mattered more to him than personal misconduct: Sex abuse might be bad, but what really mattered was being on the correct side of the Catholic civil war.

The Danneels case is useful context for thinking about the bomb that went off on an already cratered Catholic landscape over the weekend, when the former papal nuncio in the United States, Archbishop Carlo Maria Viganò, published a "testimony" accusing a raft of high Vatican officials of longstanding knowledge of the sexual crimes of Cardinal Theodore McCarrick.

Viganò's document, extraordinary in both content and tone, claims that after years of failed American attempts to get Rome to take action,

STEPHEN MCCARTHY/SPORTSFILE/GETTY IMAGES

Pope Francis in Dublin on Saturday.

Francis' predecessor, Benedict XVI, placed the already retired McCarrick under some form of sanctions — moving him out of his residence, restricting contact with seminarians, limiting public appearances. It further claims that despite being told that McCarrick was a sexual predator, Francis removed those sanctions, raised McCarrick's profile and relied on him for advice about major appointments. Oh, and it calls on Francis to resign.

As yet none of the Vatican figures named in the document have stepped forward to either confirm or deny the meat of Viganò's account. Francis himself offered only a deflecting comment on his flight back from post-Catholic Ireland. However, Cardinal Donald Wuerl of Washington, D.C., already embattled over sex abuse cover-ups in his own past, has issued a statement denying that Viganò ever communicated directly with him about restrictions on his predecessor.

Meanwhile the pope's defenders have pointed to Viganò's own anti-Francis conservatism (manifest in some of his sweeping claims) as reasons to disbelieve his charges, while noting that McCarrick appeared at many events, including with Benedict himself, in the period when he was supposedly under sanctions.

But at the same time evidence in favor of Viganò's account is trickling out — including a claim of confirmation from people close to Benedict himself. And given the distracted and ineffectual way that the last pope ran the church, it's very easy to imagine a distracted and ineffectual attempt to restrict McCarrick being subverted and ignored by the cardinal and his allies in the hierarchy.

In which case it's also easy to imagine a scenario in which Francis didn't technically "lift" those sanctions so much as acted in ignorance of them, or of their seriousness. He might have been given some knowledge, by Viganò and others, of the allegations against McCarrick but either assumed they couldn't be that bad (at this point the cardinal mostly stood accused of imposing himself on seminarians, not teenage minors) or else chose to believe a denial from the accused cardinal himself. Why? In part because of perceived self-interest: Francis needed allies, McCarrick was sympathetic to the pope's planned liberalizing push, and the pope wanted his help reshaping the ranks of American bishops.

In this scenario Francis would be guilty of self-deception and incuriosity but not as nakedly culpable as Viganò implies. And if it's easy to imagine this scenario because of the Danneels example, it's also easy to imagine because that's how things have proceeded consistently in the church since the sex abuse scandals broke: If a given predator or enabler is "on side" for either conservatives or liberals, he will find defenders and protectors for as long as events and revelations permit.

That's a major reason John Paul II refused to investigate Father Marcel Maciel, the wicked founder of the Legionaries of Christ — because the Legionaries were conservative, and apparently a great success, and that was all that mattered. It's why many conservative Catholics unwisely defended John Paul II-appointed prelates like Boston's Bernard Law in the early 2000s. It's why a notorious traditionalist priest, Father Carlos Urrutigoity, could find a welcome from conservative bishops in Pennsylvania and then Paraguay, despite a trail of abuse allegations.

Now it's why certain organs and apostles of liberal Catholicism are running interference for McCarrick's protectors — because Francis is their pope, the liberalizer they yearned for all through the John Paul and Benedict years, and all's fair in the Catholic civil war.

But the inevitable, even providential irony is that this sort of team thinking never leads to theological victory, but only to exposure, shame, disaster. Indeed, the lesson of these bitter decades is that any faction hoping to lead Roman Catholicism out of crisis should begin with purges within its own ranks, with intolerance for any hint of corruption.

Francis, alas for everyone, did the opposite. Elected by cardinals eager for a cleanup at the Vatican, he wanted to be a theological change agent instead — which led him to tolerate the corrupt Roman old guard (whose names fill Viganò's letter) and to rehabilitate liberal figures like Danneels, McCarrick and Cardinal Oscar Maradiaga of Honduras (a dubious figure with a predator among his underlings and a scandal at his seminary) who deserved the sidelines if not a penitent's cell.

Now those allies may be the ruin of his pontificate. But this doesn't mean that the pope should resign — not even if Viganò is fully vindicated. One papal resignation per millennium is more than enough. That cop-out should not be easily available to pontiffs confronted with scandals, including scandals of their own making, any more than it should be available to fathers.

Instead the faithful should press Francis to fulfill the paternal obligations at which he has failed to date, to purge the corruption he has tolerated and to supply Catholicism with what it has lacked these many years: a leader willing to be zealous and uncompromising against what Benedict called the "filth" in the church, no matter how many heads must roll on his own side of the Catholic civil war.

ROSS DOUTHAT is an Op-Ed columnist for The New York Times.

Pope Francis Embraces Silence as Calls Grow for Response to Allegations

BY JASON HOROWITZ | SEPT. 3, 2018

ROME — As a clamor builds for Pope Francis to respond to the stunning allegations by his former ambassador in Washington that he covered up abuse and lied about a meeting with a prominent opponent to same-sex marriage, the pontiff has extolled the virtues of silence.

Speaking in a Monday morning homily at the Vatican, Francis said, "With people who don't have good will, who seek only scandal, who want only division, who seek only destruction — including within the family: silence, prayer."

He added that "the truth is humble, the truth is silent" and concluded with the prayer, "May the Lord give us the grace to discern when we should speak and when we should stay silent."

So far, Francis has stuck with silence since the allegations first shook the church on Aug. 26.

Archbishop Carlo Maria Viganò, the former Vatican ambassador, accused the pope of knowing about sexual misconduct by an American cardinal, Theodore E. McCarrick, with adult seminarians years before the abuse became public. Archbishop Viganò also said that Francis lifted sanctions on the cardinal that he claimed had been imposed by his predecessor, Benedict XVI. Those allegations remain unproven.

On the day of the publication of the bombshell letter containing the allegations, reporters inquired whether the allegations were true.

"I will not say a single word about this," Francis said aboard the papal plane, returning from a trip to Ireland. "I believe the statement speaks for itself. And you have the journalistic capacity to draw your own conclusions. It's an act of faith. When some time passes and you have drawn your conclusions, I may speak."

That moment has clearly not yet come, and Benedict and other Vatican officials who may be in possession of the information to clear up the mystery — one way or the other — have followed his lead. The silence has made it exceedingly difficult to draw any conclusions.

But if Francis' rumination on the dignity of silence was intended to prompt his critics to also hold their tongues, that seemed a prayer unlikely to be answered.

Archbishop Viganò has shown no signs of letting up in his public campaign to force the pope's resignation, and his conservative allies in the United States and Rome have sounded doubts about the pope from their pulpits, conservative Catholic media outlets and social media platforms.

The pope lamented this often-hostile ecosystem in April, when he wrote witheringly in an apostolic exhortation about the tone of the discourse in the conservative Catholic blogosphere.

"Christians, too, can be caught up in networks of verbal violence through the internet," Francis said, citing vicious examples of defamation in some Catholic outlets. "Here we see how the unguarded tongue, set on fire by hell, sets all things ablaze."

But it is a conflagration that Francis himself may have facilitated.

Critics argue he has enraged conservatives in the church by disregarding traditions, but also with a leadership style that led one critic to title his book about the Francis papacy, "The Dictator Pope."

The pope's supporters instead interpret the open dissent and remarkable broadsides against Francis as a result of frustrated conservatives, unaccustomed to being out of power, coupled with a pope who is willing to give even his harshest critics much more leeway than his recent predecessors.

The notion of the pope as the embodiment of church orthodoxy emerged only in the 19th century, according to Massimo Faggioli, a professor of historical theology at Villanova University and a contributor to liberal Catholic journals.

At the beginning of the 20th century, Pope Pius X ordered a purge of Catholic theologians taking a modernist approach to teaching the Bible. Smaller purges took place under Pope Pius XII, whose papacy stretched from 1939 to 1958. But it was with the election in 1978 of Pope John Paul II, himself a theologian, that disagreements within the church took on the stigma of unholy dissent.

With Cardinal Joseph Ratzinger, later Benedict XVI, as John Paul II's doctrinal watchdog, the Vatican actively investigated and silenced theologians with a different vision of the church. When he became pope, Benedict ordered the removal of the editor of a Jesuit journal, America Magazine, because it entertained ideas anathema to conservative orthodoxy.

Conversely, Pope Francis, he said, "is not doing anything to stop" theologians. Mr. Faggioli argued that, as a Jesuit, Francis wants to foster debate so a spirit of discernment can lead people to the truth. "Francis had encouraged in the church an openness of opinions," he said.

Some of the pope's most high-profile critics have made the most of this leniency, at times challenging the very premise of papal authority.

Cardinal Raymond L. Burke, an American Vatican official who is the global leader of traditionalists critical of Francis, was a featured speaker at a Rome event in April about confusion under Francis.

In his speech on the limits of papal authority, Cardinal Burke, an expert in canon law, argued if a pope failed to act in conformity with church revelation, scripture and tradition, his actions "must be rejected by the faithful." Without specifically mentioning Francis, he argued that a pope's authority was not "magical, but derives from his obedience to the Lord," and that the actions of a "heretical or sinful" pope were "void."

Archbishop Viganò sat in one of the front rows of the event and apparently took that message to heart. While he did not hide in private settings his distaste for Francis and the direction in which he was taking the church, his going public against the pope was another matter. People who have spoken with him in the last few weeks said he did not take the decision lightly.

"He is a diplomat who was taught to be silent his whole life," said Marco Tosatti, the conservative journalist who helped him draft the letter accusing the pope. "And there was an oath that he broke doing this."

But by being so outspoken, Archbishop Viganò has also essentially ensured his protection from censure. Punishing the archbishop now would fuel speculation Francis has something to hide.

Instead, Francis has relied on some outspoken American bishops and an army of progressive Catholics online to defend him. His most active lieutenant, Rev. Antonio Spadaro, the editor of a Jesuit journal, La Civiltà Cattolica, has in the past accused American conservative Catholic bishops of damaging the church by making common cause with American evangelicals to further political interests.

Much of the critique of Archbishop Viganò has been seen through this lens, and the pope's supporters argue that any response would only give oxygen to critics who are less interested in the truth than in exploiting the sex abuse crisis to slow down Francis and his agenda.

On Sunday, Father Spadaro brought Rev. Federico Lombardi, a former papal spokesman, out of retirement and onto his journal, which is vetted by the Vatican Secretariat of State before publication. Father Lombardi immediately joined the fight, issuing a statement that same day claiming Archbishop Viganò had deceived the pope in arranging a private meeting in 2015 with Kim Davis, the county clerk in Kentucky who became a national icon for opponents of gay marriage.

The pope, however, has remained mum, preferring to let the Gospel do the talking.

"Jesus responds with silence before those 'who wanted to throw him out of the city,' " he said during a Mass on Monday, adding that Jesus' stance reflected a "silence that triumphs."

Glossary

annulment Cancellation of a marriage by the Church, on condition that it was not consummated.

apostolic exhortation A written work by the Pope that outlines policy goals without strictly defining church doctrine.

cardinal A leading church figure, chosen by the Pope, who carries out church duties and elects a successor when the Pope dies.

clericalism A culture of excessive power held by church authorities.

communion One of the sacraments of Catholicism, in which bread and wine are consecrated and shared during a church service.

decentralization The Church's practice of granting additional freedoms to local church authorities.

ecumenicism The practice of reaching out to other Christian denominations to find a common ground.

Eucharist Another term for the sacrament of communion.

evangelicalism A form of Christianity, typically protestant, that emphasizes individual salvation.

extremism Subscribing to strong religious or political beliefs.

Holy See The official jurisdiction of the papacy, considered a sovereign state by international law.

Latin The official language of the Catholic Church.

liberation theology A form of Christian teaching popular in the developing world, emphasizing social justice.

liturgy The texts and guidelines for public religious worship.

martyr A person who has died for their religious beliefs.

papacy The period of rule of a particular Pope.

papal conclave Official secret meeting of cardinals to elect a new Pope.

papal encyclical A document written by the Pope outlining how to interpret church doctrine.

papal infallibility The belief in the Pope's inability to err in interpreting Catholic teachings, invoked throughout the church's history to set limits on acceptable interpretations.

populism Political position appealing to the needs of everyday people, often used to refer to the recent rise of far-right populist political parties.

relativism The belief that values are relative rather than absolute.

religious right The combination of right-wing politics with religious values.

Roman Curia Administrative bodies making up Vatican governance.

sacrament The core ceremonies of Christian teaching.

Second Vatican Council A series of official Vatican meetings from 1962-1965 that modernized elements of Catholic doctrine.

secularism The separation of public and religious life.

sexual revolution The change in sexual norms and gender roles that took place in the 1960s.

synod An assembly of clergy.

theology Research into the nature of God or spirituality, typically by a religious institution.

traditionalist A believer in resisting change by upholding tradition.

Vatican City A city-state in Rome, including the headquarters of the Catholic Church and residency of the pope.

Media Literacy Terms

"Media literacy" refers to the ability to access, understand, critically assess and create media. The following terms are important components of media literacy, and they will help you critically engage with the articles in this title.

angle The aspect of a news story that a journalist focuses on and develops.

attribution The method by which a source is identified or by which facts and information are assigned to the person who provided them.

balance Principle of journalism that both perspectives of an argument should be presented in a fair way.

bias A disposition of prejudice in favor of a certain idea, person, or perspective.

byline Name of the writer, usually placed between the headline and the story.

chronological order Method of writing a story presenting the details of the story in the order in which they occurred.

credibility The quality of being trustworthy and believable, said of a journalistic source.

editorial Article of opinion or interpretation.

feature story Article designed to entertain as well as to inform.

headline Type, usually 18 point or larger, used to introduce a story.

human interest story Type of story that focuses on individuals and how events or issues affect their life, generally offering a sense of relatability to the reader.

impartiality Principle of journalism that a story should not reflect a journalist's bias and should contain balance.

intention The motive or reason behind something, such as the publication of a news story.

interview story Type of story in which the facts are gathered primarily by interviewing another person or persons.

inverted pyramid Method of writing a story using facts in order of importance, beginning with a lead and then gradually adding paragraphs in order of relevance from most interesting to least interesting.

motive The reason behind something, such as the publication of a news story or a source's perspective on an issue.

news story An article or style of expository writing that reports news, generally in a straightforward fashion and without editorial comment.

op-ed An opinion piece that reflects a prominent individual's opinion on a topic of interest.

paraphrase The summary of an individual's words, with attribution, rather than a direct quotation of their exact words.

quotation The use of an individual's exact words indicated by the use of quotation marks and proper attribution.

reliability The quality of being dependable and accurate, said of a journalistic source.

rhetorical device Technique in writing intending to persuade the reader or communicate a message from a certain perspective.

tone A manner of expression in writing or speech.

Media Literacy Questions

1. Ross Douthat has written many op-eds about Pope Francis, including "The End of a Catholic Moment" (page 20) and "Pope Francis in Context" (page 84). What is Douthat's basis of expertise on Catholicism?

2. Rachel Donadio's article "Cardinals Pick Bergoglio, Who Will Be Pope Francis" (page 28) is written in the inverted pyramid form. Compare the first and last paragraph. How did the author determine which information is most important to include?

3. Rachel Donadio's article "Life on the Papal Beat" (page 38) is a human interest story. What is the angle of this story, and what audience does it appeal to?

4. The article "Room for Debate: The New Pope's New Direction" (page 50) has four authors writing in response to Pope Francis' first apostolic exhortation. What is the angle or motive of each author?

5. Jim Yardley and Laurie Goodstein's article "Francis' Message Calls on Church to Be Inclusive" (page 62) is about Pope Francis' most controversial written works. Does the article demonstrate the journalistic principle of balance?

6. Examine the headline of Jason Horowitz's article "A Vatican Shot Across the Bow for Hard-Line U.S. Catholics" (page 93). How does the headline convey the religious and political conflict it describes?

7. What is the angle of John Gehring's article "Can the Catholic Church 'Evolve' on L.G.B.T. Rights?" (page 112)? How does Gehring develop this line of analysis?

8. Andrew C. Revkin's article "Tracing the Roots of Pope Francis' Climate Plans for 2015" (page 120) uses extensive block quotations. What sources does Revkin draw upon, and how do they shape the story?

9. What is the tone of Yi-Zheng Lian's article "Why the Pope Is Genuflecting to China" (page 142)? What perspective does it suggest? Compare with op-eds by Ross Douthat.

10. Examine the sources used in Jason Horowitz's article "Ten Centuries Later, a Pope and Knights Do Battle" (page 166).

11. "The Pope Causes More Pain for Priests' Victims" (page 172) is an editorial. What is the motive?

12. Jason Horowitz's article "Pope Francis Long Knew of Cardinal's Abuse and Must Resign, Archbishop Says" (page 195) quotes sources on behind-the-scenes Vatican conflicts. How does the reporter assess each source's reliability?

Citations

All citations in this list are formatted according to the Modern Language Association's (MLA) style guide.

BOOK CITATION

THE NEW YORK TIMES EDITORIAL STAFF. *Pope Francis.* New York: New York Times Educational Publishing, 2019.

ONLINE ARTICLE CITATIONS

AUSTEN, IAN, AND JASON HOROWITZ. "A Pope Given to Apologies Has Nothing for Indigenous Canada." *The New York Times*, 23 Apr. 2018, https://www.nytimes.com/2018/04/23/world/canada/pope-indigenous-apology-canada.html.

DONADIO, RACHEL. "Cardinals Pick Bergoglio, Who Will Be Pope Francis." *The New York Times*, 13 Mar. 2013, https://www.nytimes.com/2013/03/14/world/europe/cardinals-elect-new-pope.html.

DONADIO, RACHEL. "Life on the Papal Beat." *The New York Times*, 18 Sept. 2015, https://www.nytimes.com/2015/09/20/magazine/life-on-the-papal-beat.html.

DONADIO, RACHEL. "On Gay Priests, Pope Francis Asks, 'Who Am I to Judge?' " *The New York Times*, 29 July 2013, https://www.nytimes.com/2013/07/30/world/europe/pope-francis-gay-priests.html.

DONADIO, RACHEL. "Pope Is Quoted Referring to a Vatican 'Gay Lobby.' " *The New York Times*, 12 June 2013, https://www.nytimes.com/2013/06/13/world/europe/pope-is-quoted-as-acknowledging-a-vatican-gay-lobby.html.

DONADIO, RACHEL, AND NICHOLAS KULISH. "A Statement Rocks Rome, Then Sends Shockwaves Around the World." *The New York Times*, 11 Feb. 2013, https://www.nytimes.com/2013/02/12/world/europe/pope-benedict-xvi-says-he-will-retire.html.

DONADIO, RACHEL, AND ELISABETTA POVOLEDO. "Successor to Benedict Will Lead a Church at a Crossroads." *The New York Times*, 11 Feb. 2013, https://

www.nytimes.com/2013/02/12/world/europe/with-popes-resignation-focus-shifts-to-a-successor.html.

DOUTHAT, ROSS. "The End of a Catholic Moment." *The New York Times*, 16 Feb. 2013, https://www.nytimes.com/2013/02/17/opinion/sunday/douthat-the-end-of-a-catholic-moment.html.

DOUTHAT, ROSS. "The Pope and the Right." *The New York Times*, 30 Nov. 2013, https://www.nytimes.com/2013/12/01/opinion/sunday/douthat-the-pope-and-the-right.html.

DOUTHAT, ROSS. "Pope Francis' Call to Action Goes Beyond the Environment." *The New York Times*, 20 June 2015, https://www.nytimes.com/2015/06/21/opinion/sunday/ross-douthat-pope-francis-call-to-action-goes-beyond-the-environment.html.

DOUTHAT, ROSS. "Pope Francis in Context." *The New York Times*, 30 July 2013, https://douthat.blogs.nytimes.com/2013/07/30/pope-francis-in-context/.

DOUTHAT, ROSS. "Pope Francis Is Beloved. His Papacy Might Be a Disaster." *The New York Times*, 16 Mar. 2018, https://www.nytimes.com/2018/03/16/opinion/pope-francis-vatican-disaster.html.

DOUTHAT, ROSS. "The Vatican's America Problem." *The New York Times*, 2 Aug. 2017, https://www.nytimes.com/2017/08/02/opinion/vatican-conservative-catholics-america.html.

DOUTHAT, ROSS. "What Did Pope Francis Know?" *The New York Times*, 28 Aug. 2018, https://www.nytimes.com/2018/08/28/opinion/pope-francis-catholic-church-resign.html.

ELIE, PAUL. "Francis, the Anti-Strongman." *The New York Times*, 24 Mar. 2018, https://www.nytimes.com/2018/03/24/opinion/sunday/francis-the-anti-strongman.html.

GEHRING, JOHN. "Can the Catholic Church 'Evolve' on L.G.B.T. Rights?" *The New York Times*, 5 July 2018, https://www.nytimes.com/2018/07/05/opinion/pope-francis-catholic-church-lgbt.html.

GOODSTEIN, LAURIE, AND SHARON OTTERMAN. "Catholic Priests Abused 1,000 Children in Pennsylvania, Report Says." *The New York Times*, 14 Aug. 2018, https://www.nytimes.com/2018/08/14/us/catholic-church-sex-abuse-pennsylvania.html.

GOODSTEIN, LAURIE, AND ELISABETTA POVOLEDO. "Pope Sets Down Goals for an Inclusive Church, Reaching Out 'on the Streets.'" *The New York Times*, 26 Nov. 2013, https://www.nytimes.com/2013/11/27/world/europe/in-major-document-pope-francis-present-his-vision.html.

GOODSTEIN, LAURIE, AND JIM YARDLEY. "How Pope Francis' 'Amoris Laetitia' Could Affect Families and the Church." *The New York Times*, 7 Apr. 2016, https://www.nytimes.com/2016/04/08/world/europe/pope-francis-amoris-laetitia-family.html.

HOROWITZ, JASON. "As Ireland Joins Europe's Sprint From Catholic Fold, Francis Looks South." *The New York Times*, 27 May 2018, https://www.nytimes.com/2018/05/27/world/europe/pope-francis-ireland-catholic-church.html.

HOROWITZ, JASON. "Balancing Act for Pope in Egypt: Outreach to Muslims, and Speaking Out for Christians." *The New York Times*, 27 Apr. 2017, https://www.nytimes.com/2017/04/27/world/middleeast/pope-francis-egypt.html.

HOROWITZ, JASON. " 'God Made You This Way,' Pope Is Said to Have Told Gay Man." *The New York Times*, 21 May 2018, https://www.nytimes.com/2018/05/21/world/europe/pope-francis-gays-god-made-you-this-way-.html.

HOROWITZ, JASON. "Pope Defends His Myanmar Diplomacy: 'I Did Not Negotiate With the Truth.' " *The New York Times*, 2 Dec. 2017, https://www.nytimes.com/2017/12/02/world/asia/pope-francis-myanmar-rohingya.html.

HOROWITZ, JASON. "Pope Francis, After Criticism, Sends Sex Crimes Investigator to Chile." *The New York Times*, 30 Jan. 2018, https://www.nytimes.com/2018/01/30/world/europe/pope-francis-chile-abuse.html.

HOROWITZ, JASON. "Pope Francis Embraces Silence as Calls Grow for Response to Allegations." *The New York Times*, 3 Sept. 2018, https://www.nytimes.com/2018/09/03/world/europe/pope-francis-mccarrick.html.

HOROWITZ, JASON. "Pope Francis Long Knew of Cardinal's Abuse and Must Resign, Archbishop Says." *The New York Times*, 26 Aug. 2018, https://www.nytimes.com/2018/08/26/world/europe/pope-ireland-sexual-abuse-letter-vigano.html.

HOROWITZ, JASON. "Pope Francis Puts Caring for Migrants and Opposing Abortion on Equal Footing." *The New York Times*, 9 Apr. 2018, https://www.nytimes.com/2018/04/09/world/europe/pope-francis-migrants-abortion.html.

HOROWITZ, JASON. "Pope Francis Shifts Power From Rome With 'Hugely Important' Liturgical Reform." *The New York Times*, 9 Sept. 2017, https://www.nytimes.com/2017/09/09/world/europe/pope-francis-liturgical-reform.html.

HOROWITZ, JASON. "Ten Centuries Later, a Pope and Knights Do Battle." *The*

New York Times, 28 Jan. 2017, https://www.nytimes.com/2017/01/28/world/europe/ten-centuries-later-a-pope-and-knights-do-battle.html.

HOROWITZ, JASON. "A Vatican Shot Across the Bow for Hard-Line U.S. Catholics." *The New York Times*, 2 Aug. 2017, https://www.nytimes.com/2017/08/02/world/europe/vatican-us-catholic-conservatives.html.

KRASTEV, IVAN. "The Pope vs. the Populists." *The New York Times*, 2 May 2018, https://www.nytimes.com/2018/05/02/opinion/catholics-poland-hungary-populists-pope-francis.html.

LIAN, YI-ZHENG. "Why the Pope Is Genuflecting to China." *The New York Times*, 8 Feb. 2018, https://www.nytimes.com/2018/02/08/opinion/pope-china-deal-vatican.html.

THE NEW YORK TIMES. "The New Pope's New Direction." *The New York Times*, 27 Nov. 2013, https://www.nytimes.com/roomfordebate/2013/11/27/the-new-popes-new-direction.

THE NEW YORK TIMES. "The Pope Causes More Pain for Priests' Victims." *The New York Times*, 19 Jan. 2018, https://www.nytimes.com/2018/01/19/opinion/pope-victims-chile.html.

POSNER, GERALD. "How the Vatican Can Shed Light on the Holocaust." *The New York Times*, 29 July 2016, https://www.nytimes.com/2016/07/29/opinion/how-the-vatican-can-shed-light-on-the-holocaust.html.

POVOLEDO, ELISABETTA, ET AL. "Lost in Translation? Pope Ponders an Update to Lord's Prayer." *The New York Times*, 8 Dec. 2017, https://www.nytimes.com/2017/12/08/world/europe/pope-francis-lords-prayer-translation-temptation.html.

RENKL, MARGARET. "Easter Is Calling Me Back to the Church." *The New York Times*, 25 Mar. 2018, https://www.nytimes.com/2018/03/25/opinion/easter-church-faith.html.

REVKIN, ANDREW C. "Tracing the Roots of Pope Francis' Climate Plans for 2015." *The New York Times*, 31 Dec. 2014, https://dotearth.blogs.nytimes.com/2014/12/31/tracing-the-roots-of-pope-franciss-climate-plans-for-2015/.

SCHMALL, EMILY, AND LARRY ROHTER. "A Conservative With a Common Touch." *The New York Times*, 13 Mar. 2013, https://www.nytimes.com/2013/03/14/world/europe/new-pope-theologically-conservative-but-with-a-common-touch.html.

WAKIN, DANIEL J. "Cardinals Start to Ponder Subtleties of a Big Task." *The New York Times*, 4 Mar. 2013, https://www.nytimes.com/2013/03/05/world/europe/cardinal-george-of-chicago-urges-zero-tolerance-of-sex-abuse.html.

WILSON, MICHAEL. "Pope Francis, in New York, Takes On Extremism and Inequality." *The New York Times*, 25 Sept. 2015, https://www.nytimes.com/2015/09/26/nyregion/pope-francis-visits-new-york-city.html.

YARDLEY, JIM. "Prayer Meeting Shows Pope's Larger Vision." *The New York Times*, 6 June 2014, https://www.nytimes.com/2014/06/07/world/pope-francis-prayer-meeting-with-israeli-and-palestinian-presidents-shows-larger-vision.html.

YARDLEY, JIM, AND LAURIE GOODSTEIN. "Francis' Message Calls on Church to Be Inclusive." *The New York Times*, 8 Apr. 2016, https://www.nytimes.com/2016/04/09/world/europe/pope-francis-amoris-laetitia.html.

YARDLEY, JIM, AND JASON HOROWITZ. "Pope Replaces Conservative U.S. Cardinal on Influential Vatican Committee." *The New York Times*, 16 Dec. 2013, https://www.nytimes.com/2013/12/17/world/europe/pope-replaces-conservative-us-cardinal-on-influential-vatican-committee.html.

W

Y

Z

This book is current up until the time of printing. For the most up-to-date reporting, visit www.nytimes.com.